MEMORY
M A K E R S

The Complete Guide to

CREATING
HERITAGE
SCRAPBOOKS

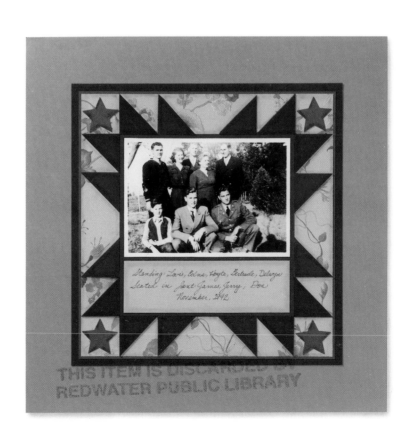

MEMORY
MAKERS
BOOKS

Executive Editor Kerry Arquette   **Founders** Michele & Ron Gerbrandt

Editor Kimberly Ball

Associate Editor Shannon Hurd

Copy Editor MaryJo Regier

Designer Andrea Zocchi

Production Artists Nick Nyffeler, Dawn Knutson

Craft Director Pam Klassen

Idea Editor Janetta Wieneke

Photographer Ken Trujillo

Photo Stylist Sylvie Abecassis

Contributing Photographers Marc Creedon, Camillo Dilizia, Christina Dooley, Brenda Martinez

Contributing Writers Darlene D'Agostino, Cindy Kacynski, Heath McKenny,

David L. Mishkin, Margaret Grove Radford

Editorial Support Dena Twinem

Special Thanks to the Editors of *Memory Makers* Magazine

Memory Makers® *The Complete Guide to Creating Heritage Scrapbooks*
Copyright© 2002 Memory Makers Books
All rights reserved.

Published by Memory Makers Books, an imprint of F & W Publications, Inc.
12365 Huron Street, Suite 500, Denver, CO 80234 Phone 1-800-254-9124 First edition. Printed in the United States.

Library of Congress Cataloging-in-Publication Data

The Complete guide to creating heritage scrapbooks / Memory Makers.
    p. cm.
  ISBN 1-892127-22-9
    1. Photograph albums. 2. Photographs--Conservation and restoration. 3. Scrapbooks. I.
Memory Makers Books.

TR465 .C63 2002
745.593--dc21

                                                                2002033764

Distributed to trade and art markets by
F & W Publications, Inc.
4700 East Galbraith Road, Cincinnati, OH 45236
Phone 1-800-289-0963

ISBN 1-892127-22-9

Memory Makers Books is the home of *Memory Makers*, the scrapbook magazine dedicated to educating and inspiring scrapbookers. To subscribe, or for more information, call 1-800-366-6465.
Visit us on the Internet at www.memorymakersmagazine.com

This book belongs to

We dedicate this book to all of our *Memory Makers* readers,
whose creative ideas, pages and techniques inspired this book.

Table of Contents

18

52

65

90

97

116

INTRODUCTION

Carmella
Teresa
D'Angelo
&
Thomas
Roland
Ryan
Married
Pennsylvania
January
1944

Like a fingerprint, our personal heritage is absolutely unique. Our family origins have a strong impact on the people we are. They form the backbone of many of our traditions and, in many cases, tie us to our religion. They influence our vocabulary, our sense of humor, and our perceptions of the world. My own family is what I call a "mixed breed" or "mutt." Each of my great-grandparents came to Ellis Island from a different place in Europe. Their children, my grandparents, did their best to assimilate to American culture, willingly embracing English and American traditions. However, they refused to give up their native foods, continuing to cook favorite dishes and hand down the secret recipes to their offspring. Today, the smell of pirogies can conjure up memories of my grandparents.

A heritage album is the perfect place to honor our ancestors and to bring together old recipes, photos, documents and stories so they can be appreciated by our families, both present and future. Heritage albums can be simple or as ornate as you wish. There are multitudes of products available to modern scrapbookers designed to lend an old-world feeling to scrapbook pages. But inventive scrapbookers can create beautiful effects with imagination, paper and a few simple tools. Within this book, you'll find more than a hundred examples of beautiful heritage scrapbook pages that are sure to pique your imagination and inspire you to create a one-of-a-kind heritage album. You'll also discover step-by-step instructions for replicating some of the special techniques featured on the pages.

While photos are an essential part of any heritage album, the facts and stories behind your family photos are equally important. Uncovering the information may seem to require accomplished sleuthing skills, but even novice detectives can ferret out the facts if they know where to look. Included in this book are clues for utilizing historical and government records and other sources, as well as ideas for interviewing family members to fill in the blanks in your knowledge of family history. A running timeline of American history will supply you with great information you may also wish to include in your album.

So, pick out your favorite pictures, pick up your favorite tools and supplies and step forward into the past. Enjoy every minute spent creating your family's heritage album.

Michele

Michele Gerbrandt

Founding Editor, *Memory Makers*® magazine

Getting Ready

The idea of beginning work on your heritage album might seem overwhelming at first: There are boxes of photos and memorabilia to sort through, questions about your ancestors to ask and, if you're a first-timer, basic scrapbooking techniques and "jargon" to learn. The first step is to take a deep breath and repeat the following: I am beginning on a fun, fascinating journey forward and, at the same time, into my past.

As with any task, creating a heritage album is much easier to address when it's broken down into tiny, bite-size pieces. Your first step is to develop a flavor or "voice" for your album. Thumb through the pages of this book for inspiration. You'll find yourself slowly beginning to develop opinions about which pages you do and don't like, as well as formulating a mental picture of the album you wish to create. Ideally, your final project will be a statement both about your heritage and your personality.

As you develop a concept for your heritage album, you'll find it helpful to visit your local scrapbook store or browse the Web to familiarize yourself with the products and supplies that are suitable for your pages. These may include patterned papers, which come in a variety of heritage-appropriate designs including dated jewelry, weathered lace, antique clocks, and worn suitcases. Other styles you might want to consider are solid, earthy-toned or muted-shades papers, transparent vellums and handmade fabric-looking patterns. Stickers, stamps, punches and die cuts are also wonderful tools for embellishing your heritage pages in a quick and easy manner. Even better, they are available in a wide variety of themes!

Your heritage pictures and memorabilia have been waiting years, perhaps generations, to find a home. They can wait a bit longer as you dream to life the perfect album: Collect product samples, clip images of heritage pages you adore, compile a folder or list of ideas, decide upon an organizational system. And then—only when you feel confident that all systems are "go"—get ready, get set and begin!

Organizing Your Photos and Memorabilia

It's time to pull your heritage photos and memorabilia out of their boxes, trunks or drawers, and start organizing them in an easily accessible manner. Something very important to keep in mind as you embark upon this process: Older photos are extremely fragile and can be easily damaged by weather or the oils on your hands, so take extra caution when handling them. Avoid direct exposure to sunlight and always wear white gloves!

Sorting

There are two primary methods for organizing your photos. The first, and most popular, is to sort your pictures chronologically. You may find it easiest to establish piles by decade, and then arrange each pile chronologically in descending order by date. Once you have completed this process, place each decade in a photo-safe, acid- and lignin-free envelope for safekeeping.

Another option is to organize your photos by theme. When applying this method, first divide your pictures into categories that represent all of the major life events—holidays, birthdays, vacations, graduations, weddings, school portraits, births—and then, as with the former method, subdivide each category chronologically in descending order by date. For convenience sake, you may want to consider creating separate piles for each branch of your family. When you're finished, store your sorted piles in photo-safe envelopes.

Storage

Ultimately, you will need to make important decisions about the long-term storage of your materials. To protect photos and documents from moisture, light and other damaging elements, you must place them in photo-safe envelopes or folders, which then must be stored inside photo-safe containers. Cardboard boxes are seldom the best storage choice for your precious materials, as they are habitually prone to collapse and may not be photo-safe. Consider investing in containers that are specifically manufactured for photo storage. While some plastics emit chemicals that are damaging to photos and memorabilia, those made of polypropylene, polyethylene and polyester are usually good choices.

Photo Duplication

You may wish to make duplicates of your heritage photos for yourself (to use in your album) and family members (to be nice). Fortunately, today's ever-expansive technology offers several quick and easy do-it-yourself options that make photo duplication a cinch!

Photo duplication machines offer one of the simplest and most economical methods. In a matter of minutes, these machines create photo-quality reprints in a variety of sizes without requiring a negative. Among other things, photo duplication machines allow you to crop your photos, correct red eye and adjust the brightness and color contrast.

It's also possible to create photo duplicates by taking pictures of the originals. This provides negatives that can be copied as often as you like. For best results, you'll need special equipment: an SLR camera, a macro lens and a copy stand. However, good copies of 5 x 7" and 8 x 10" photos can also be created by using a manual-focus 35mm or 50mm camera and sufficient sunlight. Your local camera store can provide you with more detailed information and may also rent equipment.

If you're up-to-date with digital technology, you can make your own duplicates simply by using a computer, a scanner and a compatible photo software program. Prints can be made from scanned photos and the images stored on disk or CD until further reprints are desired.

Photo Restoration

The bad news is that historical photos are often damaged long before we receive them. The good news is that they are amazingly easy to repair. While there are five primary methods of high-quality photo restoration, only three of them—digital restoration, copying and airbrushing—leave your original intact.

Digital Restoration

With this process, the picture is scanned into a computer and all blemishes are removed. Several types of new, innovative software allow you to do amazing things to your photos: remove or add people, change colors or alter physical appearances. While minor restoration work can be done by almost anyone, stains and other areas of significant damage require professional assistance, which typically costs between $75 and $200 a session, depending on the amount of repair needed.

Copying

One of the least expensive forms of photo restoration is the duplication (or taking a picture of a picture) technique. While major restorations cannot be done with this process, it's perfect for lightening stains or enhancing faded prints. Since many family photos have undetermined stability, copying is a good "insurance" method because you always receive a negative. However, be forewarned: Many professional photos are protected by copyright laws.

Airbrush

Airbrush restoration requires the skills of an accomplished artist who uses a special compressed-air paintbrush to spray paint pigments onto a copy of the original photo. Different techniques may be used to remove or add a background, combine two photos, open a closed eye, or remove an object or person from the photograph. But be careful! The more airbrushing done, the more your picture tends to resemble a painting.

Other Processes

The last two photo restoration processes, both of which require the original, are chemical (redeveloping the photo) and physical (using X-rays). Because of the expense of these procedures, they are used mostly by museums and historians.

What Your Photos Can Tell You

If you have a collection of heritage photos, no matter what size, you probably have at least a few photos about which you know nothing. You may have a guess, but it's unwise to record unsubstantiated information in your scrapbook. So pull out your magnifying glass and white cotton gloves. The answers may be right in front of you.

First, ask older family members if they have any information about the photo(s). Check the back for any writing that might offer a clue as to the time or place a photo was taken, as well as the identity of the person depicted. Some photographers mark their photos with a special seal or stamp. If your picture bears such a symbol, contact the photographer (check at the library for city directories or encyclopedias of regional photographers). He may still have records that can supply such information. Focus on year-specific details: fashions, hairstyles, car models, business signs, anything that may narrow your time frame. The littlest detail may reveal a great wealth of information. Make sure to document your sources and findings for future researchers.

Daguerreotypes
1840-circa 1860

Ambrotypes
1854-circa 1865

Tintypes
1856-early 1900s

Paper Prints
1850s-present

Supplies for Making Lasting Albums

If you want to create a long-lasting heritage scrapbook, it's essential to utilize high-quality supplies. Be wary of products that can damage photos and sensitive memorabilia. Safeguard your priceless family treasures by selecting only photo-safe materials.

Rulers and Templates Can be used to crop photos, trace decorative shapes and letters onto paper, cut patterned photo mats or create your own die cuts.

Albums Available in several styles including strap, three-ring binder and post-bound, albums come in a wide range of sizes, from 4 x 6" to 12 x 15". When purchasing an album, make sure that it's 1) an archival-quality environment for your photos and memorabilia, and 2) large enough to comfortably embrace said materials without tearing their edges and bending their corners. Page protectors should be polyvinyl chloride (PVC)–free.

Papers Today's versatile papers are used for a variety of functions, including photo accenting, backgrounds, matting and framing. However, make sure that ALL paper you select is acid- and lignin-free, as these chemicals can cause permanent photo damage by speeding up the discoloration and deterioration processes.

Pencils, Pens & Markers Journaling supplies give necessary information to pages. A rainbow of journaling pens and markers are available which come with a variety of tips. Use only pigment-ink pens for long-lasting writing.

De-acidifying Products If you wish to include memorabilia in your scrapbook, you may either choose to photocopy/scan it and then create prints (select oatmeal-colored paper for a more authentic, dated look). Or, as an alternative, de-acidify the original documents with a spray such as Archival Mist, a process which then allows them to be placed directly in your album without damaging nearby photos.

Embellishments Stickers, die cuts, stamps, punches and other decorative elements are available in a multitude of colors and styles. Many are appropriate for heritage albums—as long as they're photo-safe!

Adhesives Use scrapbook adhesives such as glue, tape and mounting corners that are labeled "acid-free" and "photo-safe." Rubber cement, white school glue and cellophane tape contain chemicals that can harm photos over time.

Memorabilia Keepers, Sleeves or Envelopes There are a number of convenient ways to safely encapsulate memorabilia in your scrapbook, including transparent plastic sleeves, keepers and pockets. Make sure the products you choose are PVC-free and made from polyethylene, polypropylene or polyester.

Making a Scrapbook Page

Every scrapbook begins with a single page, and every single page begins with a vision. Take some time to visualize your perfect heritage album before beginning construction. Keep in mind that the purpose of your page is to help preserve your memories. In order to do so in the most effective, visually appealing way possible, you need to make sure your pages incorporate at least these five basic elements: photos, journaling, complementary color, effective design and long-lasting construction!

Create a Layout

Focal Point

Choose an enlarged, matted, unique or exceptional photo for your page's primary focal point. The goal is not only to capture the viewer's attention, but also to visually ground your layout. All surrounding photos should support this central image.

Balance

Place your photos on a one- or two-page spread. Note that unusually large, bright or busy photographs may dominate the page and need to be balanced out by less busy counterparts. Move the photos around until you've achieved a look that is visually appealing to you. Remember to leave enough space for title, journaling and embellishments!

Matting

Single or layered paper photo mats focus attention and add balance to a page. Use a paper trimmer, template, decorative scissors, or just freehand-cut a mat, leaving a border around the photo.

Color

Choose a background, mat papers and design additions that complement your photos. These elements should not compete with your pictures, instead, they should help them "pop" off the page. Keep in mind that, when it comes to color, less is often more, as too much can be distracting.

Crop-n-Assemble

Cropping

Photo cropping can add style, emphasize a subject, or remove a busy background from a page. However, it is not advisable to crop a heritage photo, because doing so may inadvertently remove important sections that help define historical events. If you choose to crop heritage pictures, have duplicates made. Store the originals in a photo-safe box and only crop the copies!

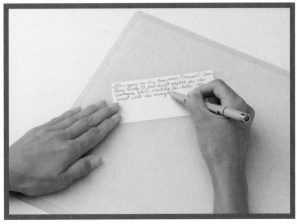

Mounting

Mount duplicates of your heritage photos using a double-sided tape or liquid adhesive to achieve a permanent bond or use paper or plastic photo corners, which come in a variety of colors and styles, when mounting original pictures. They are adhered directly to your page and allow the corners of your pictures to be tucked neatly inside. This allows you to safely remove your photos at a later date, should you wish to duplicate them.

Journaling

The stories behind your photos are details forever lost if they're not included on your page. To prevent this from happening, incorporate one—or a combination—of these simple journaling techniques:

Storytelling

Give details about those individuals displayed in the photo: Include everything from clothing, mood, conversation or background items—perhaps even the weather!

Quotes, Poems & Sayings

Search for your subject on quote-related Web sites, in poetry books, in the Bible, even on T-shirts! Or, for a more personalized effect, write your own.

Bullets

List the basics of who, what, when, where and why in bullet form.

Captions

Expand on bulleted information with complete sentences, allowing for more creative expression.

Journaling tips

- Write freehand in light pencil first, then trace with ink.

- Journal on a separate piece of paper, cut it out and mount on the page.

- Use a pencil to trace a lettering or journaling template on the page, then retrace with ink.

- Print journaling on your computer. Crop, mat and mount (or trace!) onto your page using a light box.

- Journal onto die cuts or mats, write around your photos in curved lines or turn paragraphs into shapes.

- Use the journaling questions on page 19 to help bring your photographic story to life.

Clara and Archie experienced many enjoyable weekends with my great uncle Frank and great aunt Helen. They must have been great friends to be so willing to help do dishes in the kitchen. Frank and Helen lived in South Haven Michigan and were married in 1991o.

Good Food

Great Friends

 All photos and memorabilia passed down through generations are precious and worth preserving. Among the most cherished pictures are the images portraying daily life, the bread-and-butter details of people and times long-gone. While looking at these old photos, we grow vibrantly aware that we share as many similarities with those who lived long ago as we do differences. The same day-to-day activities that tied their lives together also weave through our own, reminders of the fact that the more things change, the more they stay the same. Although the quaint one-room school-house has morphed into a giant high-tech conglomerate, school days have always been and will always be an intellectual and social beginning. Toys keep evolving, but children at play still tease and tussle. Work, whether behind a computer or behind a plow, can be both exhausting and fulfilling. Scrapbooking photos of our ancestors' daily lives reinforces our common bond and also helps us see them as the individuals they really were, caught for a candid instant. These are the very people we wish to know and remember.

U.S. population: 23.1 million. World population: 1.1 billion

The first women's rights convention meets in July in Seneca Falls, N.Y.

English painter John Everett Millais is accused of blasphemy for his *Christ in the House of His Parents*.

Herman Melville publishes *Moby Dick*.

First American chapter of the YMCA is organized in Boston.

Harriet Beecher Stowe's *Uncle Tom's Cabin* is published as a serial in an antislavery newspaper. It is published as a novel in March 1852.

Elisha Otis designs the passenger elevator.

Uncle Sam appears for the first time in a weekly comic publication.

Massachusetts passes the first mandatory school attendance law in the U.S.

Elizabeth Helen Blonn
Find design inspiration in wall-paper

For this background, Liane re-created a wallpaper pattern. Mat dark plum cardstock with forest green cardstock, leaving a ½" border on the sides. Outline with gold border stickers (Mrs. Grossman's). Center a 7¼ x 10½" piece of mauve cardstock on the green cardstock. Punch approximately 350 small telephones (Punch Bunch) from red brick paper. Trim off the receiver and outline remaining shape with gold gel pen. Layer in rows, beginning at the top and flush with the left side of the mauve paper.

Make border accents with three punched swirls (Family Treasures) laid side-by-side and accented with the negative shapes from a Heritage border punch (HyGlo/American Pin). Detail with gold gel pen. Adhere a strip of dark brown paper flush with the right side of the red border. Add strips of forest green and gold paper. Allow a strip of mauve to show and apply strips of brick red and brown paper. Continue pattern across mauve background. Run gold embroidery floss around pattern. Double mat photo and apply gold border stickers (Mrs. Grossman's). Print journaling.

Liane Smith, Gresham, Oregon

Sisters at Play
Accent a childhood page with buttons

Corina gave a sisterly black-and-white photo a feminine touch with soft accents. Print title onto ivory cardstock (Bazzill) and mount on patterned paper (Scrap Ease) leaving a ¼" border. Run sheer ribbon (Offray) through an adhesive application machine and smooth along the four edges of the cardstock. Double mat photo with clear photo corners (Pioneer). Double mat journaling and rocking horse and carriage stickers (Frances Meyer) and monogram initial sticker (K & Co.) on vellum (Bazzill). Adhere buttons (Jesse James) to corners and tie with thread (DMC).

Corina Minkoff, Cedar Grove, New Jersey

Grandma Holt Remembers

Ask a relative to record memories

For Christmas one year, Angi and her husband requested written childhood memories from their parents and grandparents. The results provided perfect scrapbook journaling. Computer print journaling on ivory cardstock. Chalk edges of cardstock and stamp with Antique Collectibles rubber stamps (Stampin' Up!). Heat-emboss heart locket stamp. For "Anice" page, chalk edges of journaling block; hand-write title (Creating Keepsakes) and journaling. Color in title with colored pencils. Mat on paper-torn pale green cardstock. Punch mat with Aaron's Arch photo corner slot punch (Emagination Crafts); double mat on pale green and rose cardstock. Oval-cut two photos; mat on rose cardstock.

Angi Holt, St. George, Utah

Journaling About Heritage Photos

An old photograph can be a window to the past. Take the time to research a bit about people or events displayed in the pictures. Journaled descriptions and stories turn two-dimensional images into compelling relatives and tales.

Some questions to consider:

- Who is in the photo?
- How old was this person when the photo was taken?
- When and where was the photo taken?
- Who took the photo and why?
- What is happening in the photo?
- What do you know about this person's life?
- Who were his parents and what did they do professionally?
- What was his religion?
- Where was he born?
- Where did he grow up?
- Where did he attend school?

- Did he have any special interests or hobbies?
- What was his profession?
- What happened historically during his life that impacted its direction?
- What insights or memories do you have of this person?
- How do others remember and describe this person?
- What characteristics do you share with this person?
- If you know nothing about this person, what do you imagine his life was like?
- What are the major differences between life then and life now?
- What feelings does this photo evoke in you?

1853

Henry Steinway and his three sons begin the New York firm of piano manufacturers.

Wellington gigantea, the largest tree in the world, is discovered in California.

Charles Lewis Tiffany establishes Tiffany and Company, a firm which remains renowned for its exquisite jewelry.

1854

The Republican Party is formed.

Large-scale immigration from China to the U.S. begins.

An electric telegraph is installed between Paris and London.

1855

Walt Whitman anonymously publishes his poetry collection, *Leaves of Grass*.

Florence Nightingale establishes hygiene standards in military hospitals.

Horseback riding by women is becoming popular. Many riding academies help women adjust to sidesaddle.

A Treasured Letter

Preserve a childhood letter

Virginia's grandfather saved a letter from 1949, preserving young handwriting and priceless childhood memories. Reduce and photocopy letter onto acid-free paper. Deckle-cut brown cardstock mat for letter and title with decorative scissors from brown cardstock. Mat again with cream cardstock. Double mat little girl photo and single mat envelope with address information written in black pen. Hand-write title with black pen. Mount letter, photos, title and envelope on patterned background paper (Hot Off The Press).

Virginia Butler, Milton, Pennsylvania

Jean Guernsey, Brookfield, Connecticut

Star

Remember a neighborhood friend

Jean captured memories of her mother's girlhood friend and the song they recorded as children. Double and single mat photos with black photo corners (Canson) on mustard yellow cardstock and patterned paper (Creative Memories). Freehand draw letters, teapot and cup and cut from brown textured paper (Keeping Memories Alive). Add journaling in black pen and song lyrics in gold pen. Accent with star stickers (Mrs. Grossman's).

Dapper Dresser
Hang overalls from a border

Corina used hangers from a sticker set (EK Success) to suspend her overalls and make a creative border for her page. Follow the steps below to create border title. Make photo corners for lower photo by cutting two ¾" blue squares in half. Mat photos. Thread blue buttons (All My Memories) with blue floss and attach to photo corners. Print journaling. Reduce die cut (Cock-A-Doodle Design) and color copy onto white cardstock. Silhouette and apply to journaling block.

Corina Minkoff, Cedar Grove, New Jersey

1. Mount border sticker on cardstock. Trim around it with scissors, following the design lines of the paper. Punch 13 holes at ¾" intervals across border strip.

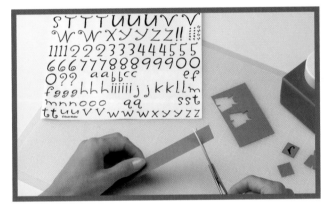

2. Cut lettering blocks. Punch overall blocks (Emagination Crafts) and squares for title. Add letter stickers (Colorbök) to title blocks and accent with pen stroke stitching.

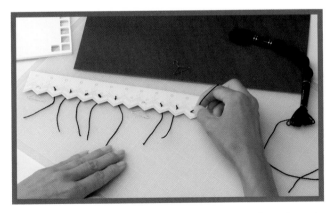

3. Knot 1½" sections of blue fiber threads and slip them through holes. Leave two holes open for the hangers, knot.

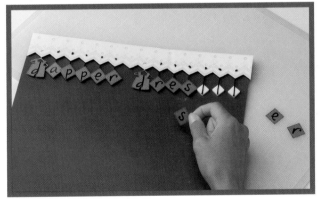

4. Adhere border sticker to black background with self-adhesive foam spacers. Pull threads downward toward bottom of page. Attach threads and letters to page with self-adhesive foam spacers. Hang hangers in holes, adhering to background.

Sue Kelemen, St. Louis, Missouri

Proud to Be a Texas Girl
Salute young patriotism

Sue captured her mother's feelings about 1940s America with a flag-inspired scrapbook page. Mat patterned paper (Robin's Nest) on ivory cardstock leaving a ¼" border. Double mat photo with blue and ivory cardstock. Write title and journaling with plum marker and mat on blue cardstock. Twist red craft wire (Artistic Wire) and adhere to mats. Accent with star buttons (Jesse James).

Shelley McLennan, St. Catharines, Ontario, Canada

Que Será Será
Press flowers for quaint border

When Shelley looks at these pictures of her mother, she says it's like watching her grow. That's why she included lyrics to the popular Italian song, meaning, "What will be, will be." Mat photos. Create mounts with Victorian corner punch (Fiskars) and mount matted photos. Print journaling on cream paper and mat. Print title on white cloud vellum paper (DMD) and mat with burgundy. Punch ¼" holes in corners and attach pink eyelets. Print journaling and triple mat. Freehand design vine embellishments and decorate page. Add pressed flowers. Adhere 2½" wide burgundy borders to salmon cardstock.

Neal

Preserve a home made heirloom

When Peggy couldn't find just the right paper for her layout, she made her own by scanning and printing clothing made fifty years ago. Mat white cardstock on blue cardstock leaving a thin border. Print title (Creating Keepsakes) and journaling onto white cardstock. Cut out title letters and back with scanned image of the sunsuit. Outline letters with blue marker and mat title block on blue cardstock. Double and triple mat photos on blue and white cardstock and scanned image of sunsuit. Reduce elephant accent from suit and adhere to page. Silhouette-cut suit and adhere to page. Freehand-cut squares from blue cardstock and scanned image; layer and top with button.

Peggy Adair, Fort Smith, Arkansas

NEAL

Neal Wayne Catlett
Born 12-28-1948
Paris Hospital, Paris, Arkansas
The overalls shown on this page were made by Lorene. She made many of his clothes and handstitched every detail.

Oregon becomes the 33rd
state in the U.S.

Dickens publishes *A Tale
of Two Cities*.

Edwin Laurentine Drake
drills the world's first oil
well in Pennsylvania.

1860

Abraham Lincoln is
elected U.S. president.

South Carolina secedes
from the Union.

Jean J. Lenoir creates the
first "horseless carriage"
with an internal combus-
tion engine.

The U.S. Secret Service is
established.

First English kindergarten
is established in Boston by
Elizabeth P. Peabody.

1861

Halls School 1925-1926

Highlight family members in a group photo

Peggy enlarged parts of a group photo to feature individuals important to her family. Seventy-seven years later, her father could still name every member of his grade school class! Scan photo and enlarge family members' faces. Cut out close-ups and mat on ivory cardstock. Double mat group photo and close-up strip on green and red cardstock; mount on patterned paper (The Paper Patch). Add journaling with white pen. Accent with punched apple (EK Success) and freehand-cut stem and leaf. Shade apple with colored pencils.

Peggy Adair, Fort Smith, Arkansas

Sing With Ringing Voices, Girls
Dress a doll in school uniform

Helen wanted a lasting record of a less-than-fashionable school uniform, so she hand-made and dressed her own paper doll. Start by cutting uniform fabric to fit 5 x 7" photo mounting sleeve (Creative Memories). Cut second sleeve to fit uniform scrap and mount on cream cardstock. Mat newspaper clipping and school song; mount with school grade reports. Mount class photo. Freehand-cut paper doll and decorate with silver, gold, black and brown pens to match school uniform. Draw music staff lines and adhere title letter stickers (Creative Memories). Journal in gold pen.

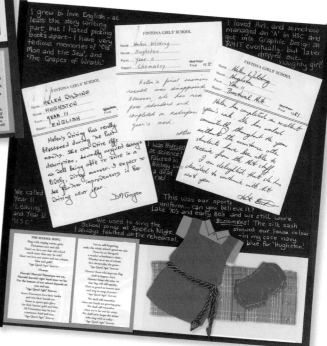

Helen Shiperlee, Thornbury, Victoria, Australia

Finally Walking
Scan clothing for background

The scanned images of a vintage baby-shoe box and Ruthann's actual baby booties wrap the photos within their time period. Double mat photos. Journal with blue and pink markers on white paper trimmed with decorative scissors. Mat with blue.

Ruthann Grabowski, Yorktown, Virginia

1862

Swiss banker Jean Henri Dunant proposes the creation of the Red Cross.

Victor Hugo publishes *Les Misérables*.

Congress authorizes the first U.S. legal tender bank notes.

Julia Ward Howe writes the "Battle Hymn of the Republic."

Theodore Thomas develops the first highly professional orchestra in the country.

1863

Lincoln issues the Emancipation Proclamation.

Jean Foucault measures the speed of light.

Union troops defeat the Confederate army at the Battle of Gettysburg. Four months later, Lincoln delivers his famous "Gettysburg Address."

1864

The phrase "In God We Trust" appears on a U.S. coin for the first time.

Jr. High

Identify family members in a group photo

Oksanna used simple lines to point out her father and his sister in old class pictures. Print journaling (Creating Keepsakes) directly on patterned background paper (Fiskars). Trim edges of photos with deckle scissors. Double mat one photo with olive green and black cardstock. Mat second photo with black cardstock cut with Majestic corner photo frame (Fiskars). Adhere title sticker letters (C-Thru) to olive green cardstock square; mat on black cardstock frame cut with M1 matting template (EZ2Cut). Adhere velvet silhouette accents (SEI). Freehand-cut identification lines. Finish with handwritten names and detailing on title block.

Oksanna Pope, Los Gatos, California

Getting photos from family members

Creating a complete album of your family may involve asking for photos or documents from distant relatives or relatives who are reluctant to part with their beloved treasures. The fastest and easiest way to get copies of the photos you need is to visit the owner. During your visit ask if you may take the photos to be duplicated. Offer to drop them off, pick them up and return them safely within a certain time frame. While visiting, show off your other work. Once family members see your dedication and the care you've taken of your own photos, they may be more willing to allow you to use theirs.

If your relatives are too far to visit or are still reticent about loaning out their pictures, try these tips:

- Tell them about your heritage album project. Describe the process of scrapbooking photo-safe albums. As an incentive, offer to send them a copy of the album when you're done.

Laura Cripe, Maineville, Ohio

Those Good Ol' College Days

Use vellum for a soft effect

Laura gave her design elements a faded, vintage look by covering them with vellum. Mount pennant and megaphone die cuts (Accu-Cut), freehand-cut jeans, shoe and cardinal, and punched stars on a black background. Journal captions with white opaque pen. Print title on vellum and mount over background. Trim photos with deckle scissors and mount them with black photo corners. Journal story with black pen.

- Offer copies of your photos in which they're interested.

- Enlist the aid of another family member who is closer to the owners of the photos. He may be willing and able to help facilitate the loan.

- Offer to pay for copying, packaging and postage.

- Promise to credit the photos' owners within your book.

- Assure that you will not display any photos the loaners do not wish included in the scrapbook.

Once you have obtained all of the photos needed, scan them so all family members can have a copy. This creates a personal e-library. If ever anything happens to the original pictures, you will be able to print another copy. This also will aid other relatives who are working on albums of their own and are searching for pictures to include.

1865

General Robert E. Lee surrenders at the Appomattox Court House, effectively ending the U.S. Civil War.

President Lincoln is assassinated.

The Thirteenth Amendment to the U.S. Constitution is ratified by 27 states, ending slavery in the U.S.

Lewis Carroll publishes *Alice's Adventures in Wonderland*.

Leo Tolstoy publishes *War and Peace*.

1866

Japan signs tariff agreements with the U.S., France, Britain and the Netherlands.

Congress authorizes the minting of the nickel.

Henry Bergh establishes the American Society for the Prevention of Cruelty to Animals (ASPCA).

Feodor Dostoevsky publishes *Crime and Punishment*.

Serbia and Montenegro form a secret alliance.

Iowa State Teachers College
Preserve both sides of a postcard

With an altered portrait sleeve, Cheri made both sides of a postcard simple and safe to read. Mat large photo with patterned paper (Hot Off The Press); mat smaller photos with green and blue cardstock. Print journaling on gray cardstock; embellish with wire and eyelets. Print years and flip instructions on gray cardstock. Create corner accents by matting stickers (Colorbök) on punched 1¼" decorative squares. Cut hole in page protector the same size as postcard. Trim a portrait sleeve (Creative Memories) to fit postcard, leaving ½" extra for flap; hold with two-sided clear tape. Print postcard journaling (Creating Keepsakes); cut mat from blue cardstock. Adhere flap of postcard sleeve between journaling block and mat.

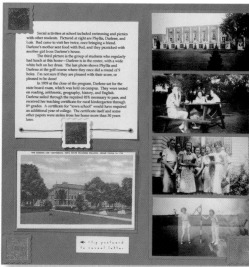

Cheri Thieleke, Ames, Iowa

Slugger
Make a manly sports tribute

Corina gave her heritage photo a masculine feel with vibrant colors and sports-inspired buttons. Print title with shadow effect on tan cardstock; add corner stickers (Me & My Big Ideas). Adhere tan cardstock to dark red cardstock, leaving a thin border. Double mat photo on olive green and dark red cardstock with clear photo corners covered with Sizzix die-cut photo corners (Provo Craft/Ellison) in dark red. Paper-tear squares from tan and olive green cardstock. Print journaling block on tan cardstock; double mat with olive green and dark red and hand-draw baseball stitching. Make holes for buttons with a pin; tie buttons (Jesse James) on with jute. Adhere buttons and jute ends.

Corina Minkoff, Cedar Grove, New Jersey

Letters to Aunt Laura and Uncle Tony
Re-create cherished correspondence

During the busy days of World War II, Joyce's parents still found time to share their love with relatives. Draw border around edge of rust cardstock with black pen. Mount printed paper (Carolee's Creations) on background cardstock. Cut postcard-size rectangles from tan cardstock; mat askew on blue cardstock. Trim photos with antique scissors (Creative Memories) and mat on rust cardstock; adhere to "postcards." Cut squares from rust cardstock with jigsaw scissors (Fiskars) and punch out hearts for "stamps." Journal excerpts from letters, postmarks and story in black ink.

Joyce Hill Schweitzer, Greensboro, North Carolina

Holle Wiktorek, Fayetteville, North Carolina

Mail for Madison's Miss Frances
Paper-tear a vintage mailbox

Holle created a mailbox to hold numerous heritage letters and envelopes. Paper-tear, chalk and assemble mailbox, mailbox door, "envelopes," post and grass on lime green cardstock. Tear and chalk title blocks and decade. Tear strips of lime green cardstock and adhere in random pattern on blue cardstock. Layer envelopes and postcards over lime green strips. Mat postcard on light blue cardstock and tear edges of mat. Add journaling to small envelopes and postmark to title with black ink. Detail post, grass and mailbox with black ink. Trace title letters from template (EK Success); color with chalk. Write the rest of title with brown marker and family name with black marker.

1867

U.S. buys Alaska from Russia for less than two cents an acre.

Britain passes the North America Act, establishing the Dominion of Canada.

Johann Strauss writes "The Blue Danube."

The Klu Klux Klan is formally organized in Nashville, Tenn.

The New England conservatory of music in Boston is founded.

Alfred Nobel patents dynamite.

Fisher of Men
Cut graphic strips for visual movement

Michelle captured her grandfather's favorite activities with a dramatic black-and-white design. Cut lure border (Creative Impressions) into strips and adhere to background paper (Robin's Nest). Print journaling on vellum and heat-emboss. Corner-slot punch black cardstock; double mat photo on black and white cardstock.

Michelle Hubbartt, Grand Junction, Colorado

Chattahoochee River, Circa 1940
Capture a fond fishing memory

Carol's father strictly followed the Army dress code and stayed in full uniform on his way home from the base—even when he stopped to do some fishing! Mount photos to brown cardstock with tan photo corners. Print journaling on tan cardstock. Punch fish (McGill) from brown and tan cardstock and adhere.

1868

New England Woman's Club is founded with the intention of promoting the efforts of women to win recognition of their rights.

Popularity of ice skating in America leads to the meeting of an American skating congress that seeks to establish it as a sport.

Christopher L. Sholes patents and names the first practical typewriter.

An act of Congress establishes an 8-hour workday.

Carol Tingley, Ocoee, Florida

Mother's Recipes

Preserve handwritten recipes

The sweet smell of a special cake or bread baking can bring back fond memories of loved ones. Remember the person and the recipe with a scrapbook page. Enlarge and color copy recipe on 8½ x 11" paper; adhere to background paper (Making Memories). Cut vellum to fit recipes and trim top edge with Cloud scissors (Fiskars). Adhere bottom and sides of vellum to background paper to form recipe pockets. Hand-write title on vellum and outline in black; adhere to recipe. Cut vellum with decorative scissors for mat, and mount photo.

Photos Connie Mieden Cox, Westminster, Colorado
Page Erikia Ghumm, Brighton, Colorado

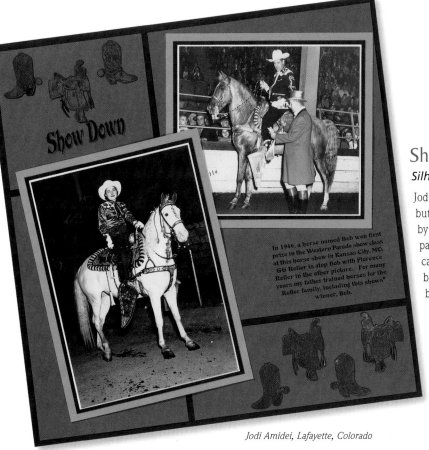

Show Down

Silhouette accents from patterned paper

Jodi loved the cowboy-themed foil paper (PrintWorks), but felt that it was too busy. She found a compromise by silhouette cropping the boot and saddle images for page accents. Print title and journaling on brown cardstock. Cut cardstock into blocks to color block black background. Triple mat photos with white, black and clay cardstock. Add foil accents.

Jodi Amidei, Lafayette, Colorado

1869

Louisa May Alcott publishes *Little Women*.

Peter Ilyich Tchaikovsky produces *Romeo and Juliet*.

The Union Pacific and Central Pacific Railroads meet at Promontory, Utah, completing the first transcontinental railroad.

H. Mège-Mouriès invents margarine.

Mahatma Gandhi is born.

1870

The Fifteenth Amendment to the U.S. Constitution is ratified, giving African-American men the right to vote. Women are still disenfranchised.

Jules Verne publishes *Twenty Thousand Leagues Under the Sea*.

A N.Y. scientist paves a road in Newark, N.J. with asphalt.

U.S. population: 39.8 million

First Vatican Council decrees papal infallibility in matters of faith.

Pasteur discovers a method that can produce unspoilable beer.

Grandpa Sam's Wheat Wine
Preserve a secret recipe

Knowing that her grandmother was a teetotaler made a wine recipe from Juli's grandfather an amusing anecdote for family history. Cut border from light blue cardstock and add beaded line stickers (Me & My Big Ideas). Color copy recipe and photo and hand-tint photo with tinting pens (Marshall). Mat recipe on brown cardstock, and photo on deckle-cut white cardstock. Print title (Creating Keepsakes) and journaling on tan cardstock. Mat title on blue cardstock.

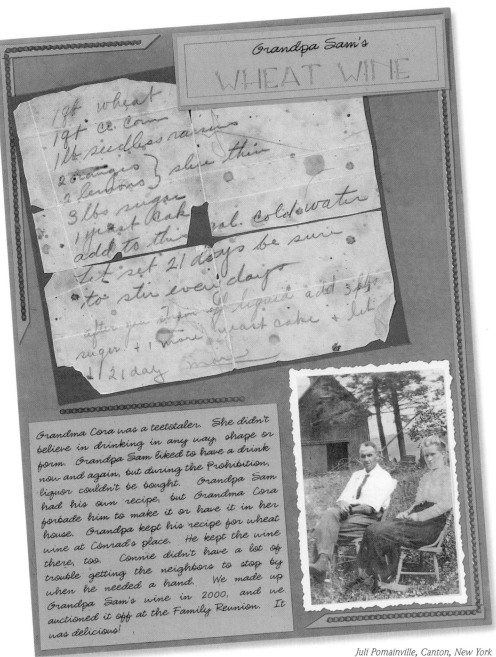

Juli Pomainville, Canton, New York

The Noblemen
Journal about an (almost) famous band

A humorous essay from her husband provided Pamela with the perfect journaling for this garage-band layout. Single and quadruple mat black and aqua cardstock and patterned paper (Sandylion). Mount on background paper (Sandylion). Print journaling (source unknown) on vellum, outline with black boxes on computer and mount to page. Print title on white cardstock, freehand-cut shields and mat on black cardstock. Add sticker accents (Sandylion).

Pamela James, Ventura, California

Violets by the Roadside
Punch colorful flowers

Liane's punched bouquet adds a dash of color to a black-and-white photo. Triple mat photo with purple, yellow and green cardstock. Cut three green squares and trim edges with wavy scissors. Punch hearts from purple, yellow and tan cardstock; slice yellow hearts in half. Punch mini sunflower (Marvy/Uchida) from purple cardstock for flower centers. Assemble one flower in each square and several for bouquet. Punch grass (Nankong) from green cardstock. Draw details on flower. Print journaling and mat on purple cardstock. Add additional flower to journaling.

Liane Smith, Gresham, Oregon

1871

The Chicago Fire kills 300 people and destroys $196 million of property.

Feudalism is abolished in Japan.

The first professional baseball association is formed.

Congress passes the Indian Appropriation Act, making all Native Americans wards of the state.

Young Love
Tear a frame's center

Paula's frame, with the torn center, draws the reader's eye immediately to her focal point. Mat photo with forest green paper. Tear out center of 5 x 6½" piece of seafoam green paper and adhere over matted photo. Attach heart brads to photo corners (Hyglo/American Pin) and apply leaf accent (Jesse James). Adhere to striped background (Northern Spy). Mat second photo and trim mat's corners. Print title with Script font on clear vellum. Mat with torn, sea-foam green paper. Print journaling on clear vellum and mat. For page's corner accents, cut two 1½" sea-foam green squares in half for four triangles. Thread green buttons (Jesse James) with multicolored metallic thread. Adhere to triangles and adhere triangles to corners.

Paula DeReamer, Alexandria, Minnesota

1872

Yellowstone National Park is established.

The Brooklyn Bridge opens.

Charles Taze Russell, a layman member of the Presbyterian Church, organizes Jehovah's Witnesses.

England and Scotland play in the first international soccer game.

1873

The Panic of 1873 begins with the failure of the Jay Cooke and Company brokerage firm and sends the U.S. into a five-year depression.

Pamela Frye, Denver, Colorado

Les & Francine
Create a psychedelic page

Swirls and bright colors make the perfect backdrop for this 1970s photo. Triple mat photo with pink and blue cardstock and gold glitter paper (Paper Adventures) rounded with a corner rounder punch; mount to patterned background paper (Wubie). Mount gold glitter borders. Cut journaling block from pink cardstock, round corners and write journaling in gold pen. Mount guitar die cut (Dayco) on blue cardstock; finish with pen and paper details.

Bud

Tell of wartime romance

Cheri made her journaling the focus of this page with delicate color and chalk shading. Mat gray cardstock on black background page, leaving a thin border. Print journaling and title (Creating Keepsakes) on tan cardstock. Shade edges with chalk and color in title with colored pencils. Mat on 4 x 11" strip of black cardstock; accent with heritage stickers (Me & My Big Ideas). Cut 1" strip of patterned paper (K & Co.) for border. Triple mat photo with black cardstock, vellum and patterned paper; mount over black cardstock and silver metallic paper (DMD) set at an angle. Attach stickers and eyelets (Stamp Doctor) to corners of mat. Handwrite initial monogram and name; mat on black cardstock and patterned paper.

Cheri Thieleke, Ames, Iowa

Once Upon a Time

Record the story of a loving courtship

Victoria made the story of her in-laws' courtship the focus of her page with a few telling photos and simple, clean accents. Print journaling (Creating Keepsakes) on gray-speckled cardstock (Club Scrap). Mat photos on purple cardstock with silver photo corners (Pioneer). Stamp swirl accents (Club Scrap), cover with silver embossing powder and heat-emboss.

Victoria Severson, Arlington Heights, Illinois

1874

1875

Life in the Logging Camps
Document historical supply prices

Jane scanned and printed an old logging camp ledger to record the 1915 prices of typical camp supplies. Mount photos and ledger copy on black page; frame with strips of wood veneer. Cut ½ x 1½" wood veneer strips and line up along left border. Layer strips with punched leaves: oak (Emagination Crafts), small maple leaf (Carl) and ash (Family Treasures). Print title and journaling onto vellum; cut out and mat on white cardstock for legibility. Adhere journaling blocks to wood veneer strips and layer strips with more punched leaves, include large maple leaf (Family Treasures).

Jane Korthase, Boyne City, Michigan

Virginia Butler, Milton, Pennsylvania

School Teacher
Include priceless memorabilia

A booklet listing the names of her grandmother's pupils inspired Virginia's elegant color scheme. Mount an 8½ x 11" sheet of patterned paper (Frances Meyer) to the left side of pale blue cardstock and a 3 x 11" strip of patterned paper (Amscan) to the right side. Layer hand-cut stem, punched birch leaves (McGill) and black ink skeletal leaf (Graphic Products Corp.) over 3" paper strip; mount printed vellum over leaves. Crop photo with deckle scissors and mat on deckle-cut brown cardstock; mat again on pale blue cardstock trimmed with shell corner punch (Marvy/Uchida). Add year and age in brown ink. Journal in brown ink on pale blue cardstock; mat on deckle-cut brown cardstock. Frame paper strips with lace border stickers (Mrs. Grossman's). Adhere memorabilia.

Sheriff

Document without photos

Colleen's great-grandmother's life could not be documented with photographs, so Colleen instead used journaling and symbols. The journaling begins with her great-grandmother's birth and ends with the tragic death of her husband, who was a sheriff. Tear top edge of burgundy paper and trim an inch off the left side so patterned paper (source unknown) border is visible. Print journaling on parchment paper (Making Memories). Freehand-cut sheriff symbol and chalk. Outline state shapes from atlas and silhouette crop. Journal with gel pen.

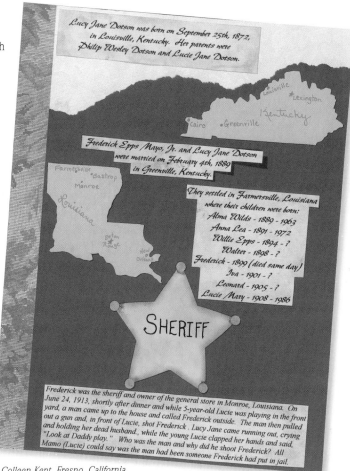

Colleen Kent, Fresno, California

What if I Don't Have Photos or Memorabilia?

You may not have a huge box of old photos or memorabilia, but with a bit of ingenuity you can get your hands on enough pieces to create a beautiful heritage album. Try these tips to amass a collection of photos, memorabilia and journaling.

- Take a look around your house. Do you have old pictures hanging on the walls or in frames on the bookshelf? Take them down and have copies made for your album.

- Contact relatives and ask for copies of their photos.

- If you have information about a person's important life events such as marriage, birth or military service you may be able to obtain government records to include in your book. (See page 66 for more information.)

- If you don't have old photos, take new ones. Tote your camera to an ancestral cemetery and snap photos of headstones. Travel to a town where your family used to live. Photocopy pictures from old newspapers that show the town "way back when." Take modern photos of the same locations from the same angles. Journal about the changes you observe.

Gather information about the time period you're including in your scrapbook. Write about important events that took place during that time. Describe a typical lifestyle for those similar to your relative.

1876

Alexander Graham Bell invents the telephone.

Sioux and Cheyenne warriors kill Gen. George A. Custer and his troops at the Battle of Little Bighorn.

Mark Twain publishes *The Adventures of Tom Sawyer.*

Peter Ilyich Tchaikovsky composes *Swan Lake.*

1877

Chief Joseph of the Nez Percé surrenders to U.S. forces and delivers his "I Will Fight No More Forever" speech.

Charles Elmer Hires makes and distributes root beer for the first time.

Thomas Edison develops the cylindrical drum phonograph.

1878

A yellow fever epidemic kills 14,000 people in the southern United States.

Bicycles are manufactured in the United States for the first time.

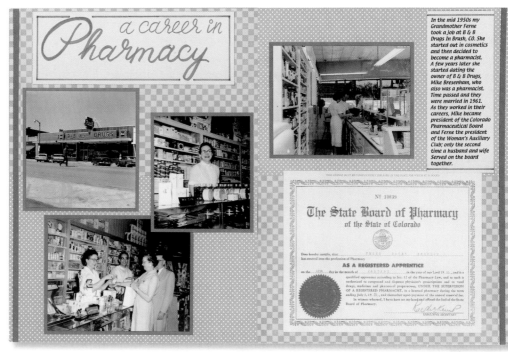

Erikia Ghumm, Brighton, Colorado

A Career in Pharmacy
Highlight career certification

Fun and funky printed papers recall the bright patterns of the 1950s. Cut checked (Making Memories) and dotted (Imaginations) papers in half and mount on cardstock, switching the position on the papers on each page. Mount thin strips of red cardstock on the outside edges of the spread. Write title in red ink and print story on ivory cardstock. Mat photos with dark green cardstock. Mount photocopy of certificate.

Dawna Vicars, Long Beach, California

Ed & Ken's Mobil®
Find vintage graphics on the Internet

Dawna sifted through extensive information on the Internet and finally found classic Mobiloil graphics for sale. Mount strip paper (Keeping Memories Alive) on speckled background paper (Keeping Memories Alive). Add "tires" cut from black cardstock with circle cutter. Single and double mat photos on red and blue cardstock and dot patterned paper with corner slot punches (McGill; All Night Media). Decorate paper doll (Ellison) with hand-drawn features and freehand-cut clothes. Print captions and mat. Print oil graphic and gas pump clip art (Microsoft Publisher) and mount.

A Lifetime of Ministry

Make a pocket page to preserve documents

A pocket page provides a safe holding place for a minister's sermons and certificates. Cut a piece of black cardstock to size of desired pocket; trim top edge with decorative ruler. Adhere sides and bottom to form pocket. Print journaling and mount on black cardstock. Write titles; mat titles and photos on red cardstock. Sponge die-cut frames (Gina Bear, Scherenschnitte Designs) with gold metallic ink. Let dry and run through adhesive application machine. Mount one frame atop matted photo; mat other frame on red cardstock and cut apart for pocket accents. Punch additional accents (All Night Media) from blue paper. All captions in gold ink.

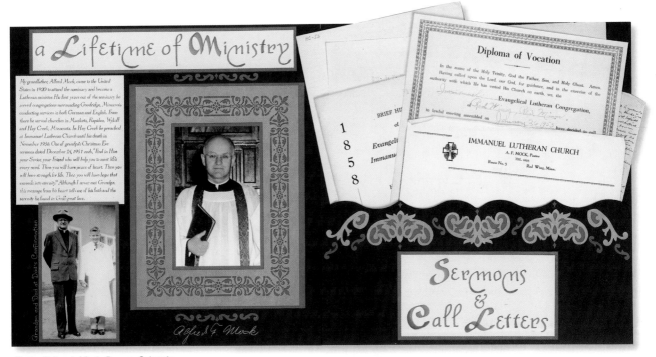

Photos Deborah Mock, Denver, Colorado
Page Erikia Ghumm, Brighton, Colorado

Say Cheese

Preserve a career keepsake

A piece of cheesecloth adds dimension and texture to a layout of an unusual career. Mount striped paper (Family Archives) on black cardstock, leaving a thin border. Adhere sticker strips (Me & My Big Ideas) and photo corners to striped paper. Cover orange cardstock square with cheesecloth and add a string bow. Double mat photos with red cardstock and deckle-cut tan cardstock. Print journaling and mat on tan cardstock.

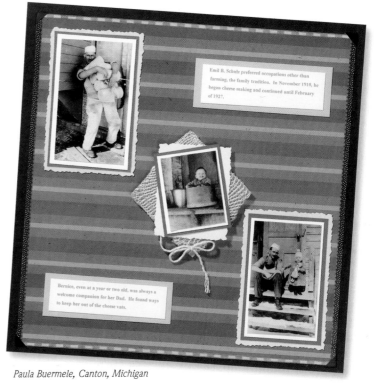

Paula Buermele, Canton, Michigan

CELEBRATIONS

My Parents' Wedding

June 8th, 1957

Celebrating special occasions was just as important to our ancestors as it is to us today, perhaps even more so. Life could be difficult in days gone by with long hours of hard labor and mundane chores. Special occasions were highly anticipated.

They were a chance to relax, rejoice and regain strength from the ties of friendship and family. Then, as now, birthdays were a celebration of the miracle of birth and recognition that each yearly milestone brings growth. Graduations taught the meaning of the word "bittersweet," as we close one door and open another. Weddings were eternal proof that each heart can find its perfect match. Scrapbooking about our ancestors' celebrations reminds us to treasure and record our own celebrations and to take the time for rejoicing and sharing all that we are with all whom we love.

1879

An Act of Congress grants women lawyers the right to argue before the Supreme Court.

Thomas Edison and J.W. Swan independently invent the first practical electric lamp.

Frank W. Woolworth opens his first successful store in Lancaster, Pennsylvania.

1880

Auguste Rodin exhibits his sculpture *The Thinker*.

U.S. population: 50.1 million

First American branch of the Salvation Army is established in Philadelphia.

The Pirates of Penzance opens in London.

1881

President James Garfield is shot.

Booker T. Washington founds the Normal and Industrial Institute for Negroes (eventually Tuskegee Institute).

P.T. Barnum and J.A. Bailey organize their circus.

The First Birthday
Include an original baby book

Deidre's grandmother carefully crafted a baby book to tell the story of her son's first year. Deidre was able to preserve pieces of the baby book in her own heritage scrapbook. Freehand-cut line accents from textured burgundy cardstock. Mount pieces of baby book. Mount old photos with clear photo corners (Creative Memories).

Deidre Justin, Richmond, Virginia

Jodi Amidei, Lafayette, Colorado

Birthday Girl
Add shine with metallic paper

The border gives luster to this otherwise simple layout. Mat sage cardstock with dark green cardstock. Cut four strips, two wider than the others, of gold leaf (Amy's Magic). Adhere strips perpendicular to each other. Double mat photos with white and red. Overlap and adhere. Cut tags from template (Accu-Cut) and mat. Punch holes in tops for green hemp string. Print title (D. J. Inkers); color in using various metallic-colored gel pens. Print journaling.

Barbara and Katherine Kraemer

Create stained-glass frames

A stained-glass frame can add color and context to a first communion page. Color copy heritage photos to the desired size. Follow the steps below to create the frames.

Julia Wilson, Wellington, Colorado

1. Freehand draw stained-glass pattern on paper the same size as black background. Refer to stained-glass pattern books for design inspiration.

2. Lay the white pattern over the black background paper on a cutting mat. Use a craft knife and a ruler to cut out each opening in the design. Save the scraps as patterns for the colored vellum pieces.

3. Using the scrap pieces as patterns, cut out colored vellum pieces which are slightly larger than the scrap pieces. Mount the vellum pieces to the back of the cut frame.

1882

1883

1884

Graduation

Color copy photo in its original frame

When Cheri color copies heritage photos, many times she keeps them in their original frames because the antique frames are so beautiful. Mat color copy with green patterned paper (Anna Griffin) and adhere to background (Anna Griffin). Print title (Creating Keepsakes). Detail with gray and gold chalk. Tear title block's edges and mat with brown strip, tearing its edges. Tear strips of green patterned paper and brown cardstock for right side. Chalk edges of patterned paper with brown. Adhere glasses, hat and pocket watch stickers (Creative Memories) to squares of paper, chalking edges with green. Adhere gold brads to brown strip. Print name and dates and journaling. Tear edges of journaling block and chalk with brown. Mat with green suede paper (Wintech).

Cheri Thieleke, Ames, Iowa

A Father's Message
Create your own background paper

Peggy made her grandfather's message to her father the focus of this layout with homemade background paper and an enlarged copy. Photocopy message several times. Cut out images and layer them on scanner; scan and print out to create background paper. Print title and journaling directly onto background paper. Enlarge and photocopy message again; print and cut out message. Mat on white cardstock. Double mat photo on black and white cardstock.

Peggy Adair, Fort Smith, Arkansas

Litton High School Prom 1966
Accent with paper-torn roses

Holle created a nostalgic atmosphere with soft-hued roses. Mat photo with red cardstock; mount on blue background cardstock. Tear title block and "prom" letters from lettering template (EK Success); detail with black pen. Adhere sticker letters (Provo Craft) to title block and numbers at the bottom of the page. Tear leaves and roses. Chalk edges of rose layers. Gently fold up edges of rose layers for a 3-D effect. Finish with journaling in silver pen.

Holle Wiktorek, Fayetteville, North Carolina

1885

Gottlieb Daimler builds the first motorcycle.

Skirmishes begin between Russian and Afghan troops at the border.

Louis Pasteur saves a young boy's life with his new rabies vaccine.

Weightlifting strongman William B. Curtis is reported to have hoisted 3,239 lbs., with a harness.

Washington Monument is dedicated. It is 585 feet high and the top is accessible by elevator and 898 steps.

August 14, 1943

1886

The Statue of Liberty is dedicated.

The art of stained-glass windows is revived by John LaFarge with his work *Red and White Peonies*.

The first Tournament of Roses is held in Pasadena, California.

After police attack striking factory workers, a riot breaks out in Haymarket Square in Chicago. A bomb kills seven policemen.

My Grandparents on Their Wedding Day
Decorate with meaningful embellishments

When Liane was deciding how to embellish her page, she went straight to the source; her grandmother provided her not only with details about the wedding bouquet but also with buttons from her own sewing stash. Triple mat photo on dark blue and ivory cardstock; mat again on patterned vellum (source unknown). Print journaling on tan cardstock; mat on dark blue cardstock. Create top embellishment by punching two super jumbo ferns (Punch Bunch) from dark green cardstock; add pearl flower buttons (Jesse James). Create journaling block embellishment with two punched ferns from dark green cardstock and pearl flower button. Create corner embellishment with several jumbo and large ferns (Martha Stewart) punched from dark green cardstock. Punch decorative corner with heritage border punch (Hyglo/American Pin) from burgundy cardstock and add negative pieces to stems. Punch hawthorn leaves (Emagination Crafts) from light, medium and dark blue cardstock; repunch to cut off stem and bottom leaves. Interlock hawthorn leaves at the bottom and layer to create flowers. Chalk edges and accent flowers with pearl buttons.

Liane Smith, Gresham, Oregon

Mr. & Mrs Osetek

Jimmie Lynn DeBerry, Albuquerque, New Mexico

Mr. & Mrs. Osetek
Accent layout with keepsake

Adding a keepsake to this simple layout doubles the sentimental value. Inside the memorabilia pocket (C-Thru Ruler) rests the "something-new" necklace the bride received on her wedding day. Double mat portraits and adhere to background (K & Co.) Use lettering template for captions and embellish with corner punch (Carl). Mat with black.

Sharon & Leonard
Punch a flowery corner decoration

Erin used a duo-tone, complementary color scheme to create an elegant layout. Punch rose border (All Night Media) at corners of cream paper; mat on mauve cardstock, leaving a thin border. Adhere ¼" mauve strips for border. Add mauve triangles to each corner. Triple mat photo on cream and mauve cardstock; mount on torn rose mulberry paper. Print title and date on cream cardstock, mat on mauve cardstock and emboss with rose quartz embossing tinsel (PSX Design). Add ribbon rosettes at corners and gathered together for decorative bouquet.

Erin Soule, North Battleford, Saskatchewan, Canada

1887

1888

1889

50 Years of Life and Love
Craft a wedding present

When Mary Faith created an album for her in-laws' golden anniversary, she started it off with a golden gift page. Mount printed vellum (Whispers) over black cardstock. Cut two 3 x 12" strips of cream cardstock. Double mat strips with metallic gold paper (Paper Adventures) and black cardstock; mount in a cross on background. Double mat photo with gold metallic paper and black cardstock. Print journaling on cream cardstock; double mat on gold metallic paper and black cardstock. Adhere silk flowers to upper left corner of page.

Mary Faith Roell, Harrison, Ohio

Cheri O'Donnell, Orange, California

1910 Ludmilla Szymanska and Izydor Brudzinski
Keep focus on photo with simple layout

Nothing distracts the eye on this simple, elegant layout. Mat photo with black paper. Use the scalloped design of the lace patterned paper (Frances Meyer) as a guide to create frame. Detail black mat with gold gel pen and adhere framed photo to rose background paper (Hot Off The Press). Freehand-cut rings from gold paper. Print title, mat with black and detail frame's corners with gold gel pen.

A Marriage Blooms

Pull accent inspiration from photos

By reading an old newspaper clipping, Laura was able to find out her parents' wedding colors—and embellish appropriately. Print journaling on vellum. Mount photos, invitation and journaling with clear photo corners on patterned background paper (Colors by Design). Color copy newspaper clipping and mount on page. Create ribbon flowers out of yellow and aqua ribbon by sewing a gathering stitch up one side of each ribbon. Gather ribbon, stitch ends of ribbon together and secure thread.

Laura Cripe, Maineville, Ohio

Other Sources of Genealogical Information

After you've exhausted all of the traditional sources for genealogical information, you'll probably discover that you still have some bare branches on your family tree. But how in the world do you go about filling in the blanks?

Beyond the myriad of official government records you've been poring over, there are a number of other sources to search. By now, you know where and when your ancestors lived, so seek out the town's publications printed while they were still alive.

Almanacs are a great source. They'll tell you who owned the land, who ran the town and perhaps who worked for whom. If you know what your ancestors did for a living, track down the companies' business records. Make a trip to the cemetery to obtain the dates of their births and deaths (and perhaps even learn a little bit about their personalities, if the epitaph is creative!). These are the little details that make a family tree more than just a litany of dates.

1890

New York's first moving-picture shows appear.

U.S. troops kill 200 Sioux at the Battle of Wounded Knee.

Sequoia and Yosemite National Parks are established in California by the federal government.

1891

Whitcomb Judson patents the zipper.

Construction begins on the Trans-Siberian Railroad.

Physical education professor James Naismith invents basketball as an indoor substitute for baseball and football.

Architect Stanford White designs Madison Square Garden in New York City.

1892

Peter Ilyich Tchaikovsky composes *The Nutcracker Suite.*

Ellis Island opens to immigrants.

The first gasoline-powered automobile is constructed.

Here Comes the Bride
Re-create a stained-glass window

For her parents' 35th anniversary, Danielle made them a new wedding album with archivally safe scrapbook supplies. Mount photo to black cardstock with clear photo corners. Adhere title sticker (Me & My Big Ideas) to white cardstock block; mat on purple cardstock. With a paper trimmer, cut 1 x ½" rectangles from various colors of cardstock. Adhere to right side of page mimicking the stained-glass window pattern. Cut off rectangles at the upper and lower edges of the page.

Danielle Diak, Parker, Colorado

Marriage in a Buggy
Document an unusual ceremony

Peggy's grandparents ran into the preacher on the way to their wedding, and he married them right there in the road! Print out journaling on vellum; mat on gold metallic paper (Daler-Rowney-Canford) and mount on patterned background paper (Family Archives). Resize, scan and print marriage license; double mat on gold metallic paper and burgundy cardstock. Scan and print copies of photos. Oval-cut smaller photo and mat on burgundy cardstock. Cut an oval frame from cardstock for mat for larger photo; mount atop photo and then mat again with gold metallic paper and burgundy cardstock. Finish with buggy sticker (Creative Memories).

Peggy Adair, Fort Smith, Arkansas

Alex Bishop, Honolulu, Hawaii

Wed

Stamp a bouquet

Alex layered these stamped rose images to resemble the bouquet. See the instructions below for the technique. Mat main photo with gray cardstock and adhere to burgundy background. Use Floral stamp (Sugarloaf Productions) for background of announcement mount. Adhere black photo corners to mount. Copy news announcement and mount. Mount two photos on background with black photo corners. Adhere two thin strips of gray cardstock to bottom of right page. Use green and red calligraphy pens for title and date.

1. On white paper, randomly stamp as many leaf, bow and rose images (any color) as you desire. Keep in mind that the more depth you wish the page to have, the more images you will need.

2. Silhouette crop around the stamped images with scissors.

3. Layer roses, bows and leaves alternately around the page's four corners, until you achieve a desired look. Mount images in place with self-adhesive foam spacers for added dimension.

Newlyweds

Use photo scraps for mats

For a vintage effect, Cheri matted her title with the cropped portion of her grandparents' photo. Create pink photo mount with corner punch (Family Treasures) and mat with dark blue, leaving ¾" border on the right side. Decorate border with strip of pink paper embellished with Scallop border punch. Mount photo and adhere to striped brown background (Frances Meyer). Cut title letters using Invitation font (Brodersbund) as a template. Double mat with cropped portion of photo and dark blue paper. Use Hannover corner punch (Emagination Crafts) to make mount for next photo. Decorate mount's corners with pieces from Baroque corner punch (All Night Media). Use negatives from corner punch to embellish page corners. Oval crop next photo and mat with navy. Apply Crown border punches (McGill) to top and bottom. Trim "wedding" journaling block and apply ribbon. Use Scallop border punch (All Night Media) to embellish "reception" journaling block. Make mount with corner punch. Print center journaling on vellum.

Cheri Thieleke, Ames, Iowa

Legacy of Love

Include an important document with a pull-out

When Susan received a copy of her grandparents' marriage certificate, the false ages on the document became part of her journaling. Cut photo mat from pink cardstock with Victorian scissors (Fiskars); double mat photo on cut pink cardstock and burgundy patterned paper (Hot Off The Press) with crochet rose photo corners (Fiskars). Trim title (Cock-A-Doodle Design) with Victorian scissors; mat on burgundy patterned paper. Mount photo and title to background patterned paper (Hot Off The Press). Print journaling on vellum. Tear out journaling; double mat on corsage patterned paper (Fiskars) and burgundy patterned paper cut with wide Victorian scissors (Fiskars). Write year and initial letter of journaling with Hot Foil pen (Staedtler) and lettering template. Cut notch in right-hand page. Copy marriage license; mat on ivory cardstock. Adhere wire-edged ribbon bow to pull-out and slide pull-out behind right page in page protector.

Susan Shute, Beaver Dam, Wisconsin

1896

Halloween
Use Harry Potter font for gothic effect

Although Brandi's title lettering lends a sense of Halloween gloominess to her page, her journaling speaks nostalgically of the simpler times characteristic in her father's childhood. Double mat photos and adhere to striped background (Family Archives). Print journaling on light brown paper. Tear edges and mat with dark brown. Use a pin to poke holes in the top corners and attach spiral wire. Adhere with self-adhesive foam spacers. For title, use Harry Potter font to print letters. Cut them out and use them to trace title onto light brown paper. Silhouette crop letters with craft knife. Adhere to dark brown strip accent with fibers (On the Surface); adhere. Freehand-cut pumpkins and chalk. Add punched leaves (EK Success) and chalk. Adhere pumpkins with ¹⁄₁₆" and a ¹⁄₈" self-adhesive foam spacers.

Brandi Ginn, Lafayette, Colorado
Photos: Helen Bryant, Aurora, Colorado

1897

Pennie Stutzman, Broomfield, Colorado

July 4th
Create star-punched patriotism

Pennie's layout depicts the "down-to-earth kind of style" that was ever-present during the Depression. For lower border, punch out small stars from strip of navy paper with hand punch (Fiskars). Mat strip on red vellum and apply heritage border stickers (Me & My Big Ideas). Apply border stickers to top. Mat photos, embellishing borders with strips of double-sided marble paper (Westrim Crafts) and a diamond border punch (McGill). Apply heritage stickers (Me & My Big Ideas) to bottoms of mats. Decorate heart die cut (Deluxe Cuts) with small and medium heart punches (McGill). Embellish bottom of heart with heritage border stickers (Me & My Big Ideas). Mat top of heart with red vellum. Embellish title lettering and date numbers with star hand punch. Print journaling on white paper.

Thanksgiving 1961

Use silhouette to identify subjects

By using a silhouette to identify this photo's subjects, Victoria avoided confusing readers with a caption of names that runs for miles. See below for instructions. Print title (Creating Keepsakes) and name chart. Using the Club Scrap Heritage kit, mat photo, silhouette, title and journaling and adhere to background. Punch red, white and brown maple leaves (Emagination Crafts) and adhere as desired.

Severson ~ Wulf ~ Holt Family Portrait
The Wulf Home on Cove Road, Sturgeon Bay, Wisconsin

1. Spike (Zileen) Reynolds Wulf
2. Porky Wulf
3. Marie Ferguson, Bob Ferguson's mother
4. Lawrence Allen Severson
5. Beverley Marilyn (Moore) Severson
6. Robin Anderson
7. Lynn Murphy
8. Suzy Anderson
9. June Holt Murphy
10. Bob Murphy
11. Marie Anderson
12. Evert Anderson
13. Barb Wulf
14. Deedee Anderson
15. Captain Carl Arlum Holt
16. Peggy Murphy
17. Zileen Murphy
18. Ricki Anderson
19. Peachy (Marion) Reynolds Severson
20. Ranson (Ranny) Severson
21. Pat Murphy
22. Don Severson
23. Cap (Thomas) Wulf
24. Steve Severson
25. Todd Wulf
26. Scott Allen Severson
27. Aggie Anderson Severson Holt
28. Bruce Arlum Severson

Victoria Severson, Arlington Heights, Illinois

1. After mounting your photo on background scrapbook page, overlay tracing paper on photo and gently trace the silhouettes of each person appearing in the photo.

2. Remove the tracing paper from the top of the photo. For easy referencing, number each of the figures silhouetted on the tracing paper in chronological order. On your journaling block, add the numbers and corresponding names of those individuals.

3. Photocopy the tracing paper, and enlarge or reduce its size as needed. Use a paper trimmer to remove extraneous edges around the paper.

1898

The Spanish-American War formally begins in April and ends in December with the Treaty of Paris.

Public outcry against meat results in First Food and Drug Act being passed.

The United States annexes Hawaii.

1899

Claude Monet begins his series of water lily paintings.

The Philippine Islands rebel against U.S. rule.

The Boer War between British and Dutch settlers begins in South Africa.

1900

U.S. population: 75.9 million

International Ladies' Garment Worker's Union is founded in New York City.

U.S. life expectancy: 48 years for men, 51 years for women.

L. Frank Baum publishes *The Wonderful Wizard of Oz*.

Family Tradition

Deck the walls with miniature copies of photos

Peggy re-created her grandparents' living room to capture joyous family holidays. Scan, reduce and print out copies of family photos; mount to patterned background paper (Daler-Rowney Canford Paper) and "frame" with stickers (Creative Memories, Me & My Big Ideas, Mrs. Grossman's). Double mat color photos with green cardstock and patterned paper (Hot Off The Press). Print journaling; mat on green cardstock. Hand-cut table, table legs and tree from colored cardstock. Edge table with lace border stickers (Mrs. Grossman's). Decorate tree with stickers (Provo Craft). Freehand-cut packages from patterned papers (Daler-Rowney-Canford Paper, Hot Off The Press, Provo Craft) and decorate with punched ribbons (Marvy/Uchida) of various colors. Accent with clock and stove stickers (Frances Meyer).

Peggy Adair, Fort Smith, Arkansas

Family Christmas Cards
Preserve heritage holiday cards

Christmas cards capture children's ages and priceless holiday excitement. Trim cards with decorative scissors (source unknown) and mount on green cardstock. Print out journaling and years on tan cardstock; mat with green and red cardstock. Cut title with dot lettering template (EK Success) from patterned paper (Paper Patch) and red cardstock. Mount over red raffia (Paper Adventures). Silhouette cut poinsettia patterned paper for border and decorative accents.

Annalia Romero, Silverdale, Washington

I Believe in Santa
Tie together cardstock blocks

Mount black cardstock blocks on gray cardstock. Mount photo. Cut title from gray cardstock with lettering template (Provo Craft). Print rest of title on vellum; cut out strips with words and mount over larger title words. Push decorative brads (Boxer Scrapbook Productions) through blocks and background cardstock; push down bard ends on back of cardstock. Pull embroidery floss through brad holes; tie off on back side.

Angela Marvel, Puyallup, Washington

IN TIMES OF WAR

My Army Days

Eisenhower visits Fort Meade 1951

Confident early days...

Jan. 6, 1951   COB-6   WAID DOBTON
FORT DEVENS   AYER, MASS.

The stories of service to country are important memories to capture in heritage scrapbooks, for these are the times when ordinary people do extraordinary things. Accordingly, military duty is rich with sights, sounds and symbols that create compelling pages: Youthful pride shines from a formal portrait taken in uniform beside the Stars and Stripes. Camaraderie is displayed in candid photos of military buddies doing chores. Honor is reflected in the weathered patina of medals won at great personal sacrifice. Grit and determination are illustrated in news clippings of women working in homefront factories. The stories behind the photos are ripe for journaling, and as compelling as the faces in the pictures. Scrapbooks that tell the stories of our loved ones' military service are living, lasting memorials and fitting reminders that our veterans have forever earned the thanks of a grateful nation.

1901

When President William McKinley is assassinated, Theodore Roosevelt becomes president.

Significant oilfields are found in Texas.

King C. Gillette releases a safety razor with a disposable blade.

1902

Congress authorizes construction of the Panama Canal.

Joseph Conrad publishes *The Heart of Darkness*.

Ida Tarbell's *History of the Standard Oil Company* begins an era of muckracking journalism.

1903

The Wright brothers fly the first manned, motorized airplane.

The first teddy bears, named after President Theodore Roosevelt, appear.

Henry Ford establishes the Ford Motor Company.

Dear Mother
Accent drab layout with strips of color

The strips of torn, muted blue paper make the sepia-toned war photos a bit brighter. For background, tear light brown paper's edges and mat with darker brown cardstock. Layer strips of torn blue paper with light brown paper for right-side border. Apply clear photo corners to photos, matting one with blue paper. Adhere correspondence. Print journaling on white paper. Apply Jolee's Boutique writing-themed stickers (EK Success), triple matting the inkwell and pen.

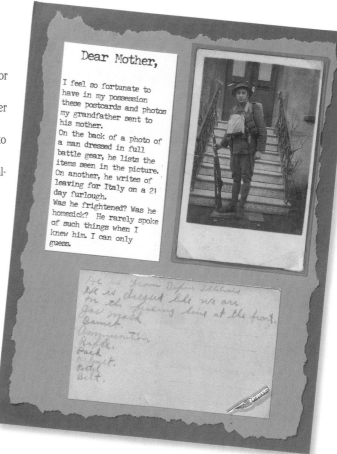

Lynne Rigazio Mau, Channahon, Illinois

Last Letter Home
Reprint letter's contents on vellum

Reprinting the letter made it possible to read its contents. Juli's use of the reduced, color-copied original as a background lends a feel of authenticity. Mat photo with torn, clear vellum using foam mounting adhesive. Attach to second mat of patterned paper (Design Originals) with green ribbon. Layer color copies as desired on green background. Adhere a block of torn clear vellum over center. Reprint letter on clear vellum and tear edges. Adhere it over the previously adhered block of clear vellum. Print journaling on clear vellum and mat. Print title on clear vellum and mat. Crop and adhere remaining photos. Adhere green ribbon along borders.

Juli Pomainville, Canton, New York

Letters From Home
Symbolize correspondence with postal-themed products

Jodi's grandmother diligently kept in touch with many WWI soldiers. Jodi found correspondence-themed paper (Design Originals), stickers (Stampa Rosa) and stamps (Hero Arts) to aptly tell the story. Triple mat photos with white, olive and linen cardstock. Cut two blocks of postcard paper and double mat with linen and olive cardstock. Print journaling on linen paper and adhere to dark green background. Print title on linen paper. Mat with olive cardstock, adhere to background and apply stamp sticker. Stamp olive cardstock with postage-stamp rubber stamp. Cut into blocks and fill in negative space. Cut linen blocks to also fill in negative space. Punch ⅛" holes in title, journaling and linen blocks to apply pewter brads. Apply postage-stamp stickers.

Jodi Amidei, Lafayette, Colorado

1904

J.M. Barrie publishes *Peter Pan*.

The New York City subway begins service.

Woman arrested in New York City for smoking a cigarette while riding in an open automobile.

1905

Albert Einstein proposes the special theory of relativity.

Number of registered automobiles rises to 77,988, as compared to only 300 ten years ago.

Mrs. Winslow's Soothing Syrup, popular for easing a baby's teeth pain, is shown to contain morphine.

1906

Upton Sinclair publishes *The Jungle*.

Marie Curie becomes the first female professor of the Sorbonne.

The most destructive earthquake in U.S. history kills 700 people, leaves 500,000 homeless and damages $400 million worth of property in San Francisco.

Lieutenant Robert J. Wourms

Create a military background

Sarah scanned in patches from a military uniform to create background paper and accents for a patriotic page. Double mat photo with red and blue cardstock. Scan and print newspaper articles on acid-free paper. Accent with scans of medals and patches.

Sarah M. Fisher, Greenwood, South Carolina

World War II

Make a timeline

This page idea, a history project in which Stephanie used a scrapbook format, adds a sense of context to WWII heritage albums. Adhere a 1¾" strip of cream paper to top and bottom borders of brown background. Cut title from patterned paper (Hot Off The Press) using letter punches (EK Success). Silhouette war images from patterned paper (Hot Off The Press) and apply to layout as desired. Apply star nailheads (JewelCraft) to lower border. Create timeline with strips of gold vellum. Print captions on cream paper and tear out. Adhere sequentially to timeline. Print years and mat with freehand-cut designs from clear vellum. Detail with brown pen.

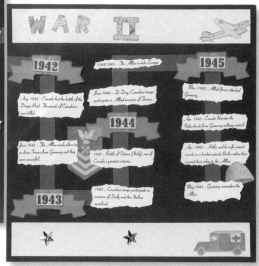

Stephanie McKean, Ajax, Ontario, Canada

Alma A. Holt

Preserve a priceless family record

Angi reduced, color copied and bound her grandfather's World War II journal to keep in her scrapbook. For right page, mat patterned paper (NRN Designs) on brown cardstock, leaving a thin border. Double mat photo on brown and tan cardstock with tan photo corners (Boston International). Silhouette cut seal of patterned paper and slip photo underneath. Print title on tan cardstock; color with pencil and mount on foam spacers for depth. Mat title on brown cardstock. To create pocket, accordion fold cardstock in ¼" folds until desired pocket thickness is achieved. Wrap folds in cardstock and mount to background paper. Punch squares in the corners of cardstock for pocket, tie with strips of brown cardstock and adhere to folds to make pocket. Mat group photo with tan photo corners on tan cardstock and mount on pocket. Paper-tear top border of pocket and add silhouette-cut boots from patterned paper. Finish with journaling in brown pen.

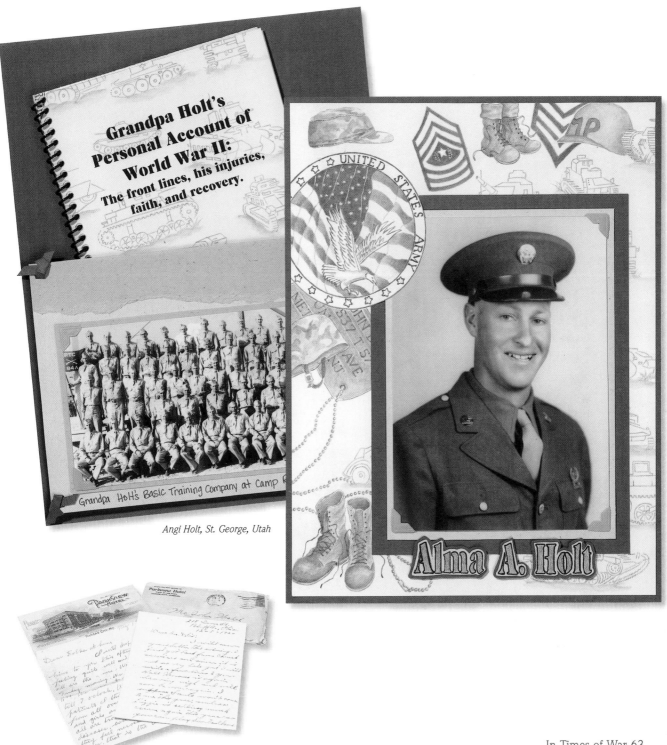

Angi Holt, St. George, Utah

1907

Pablo Picasso paints *Les Demoiselles d'Avignon*, effectively beginning the Cubist movement.

Mother's Day is observed for the first time.

Thomas Hunt Morgan proves that chromosomes influence heredity.

1908

Ford's Model T automobile hits the market for $850.

General Electric patents the toaster.

Approximately 8,000 movie houses, or "nickelodeons," exist in U.S. Movie tickets cost 5 cents.

1909

The National Association for the Advancement of Colored People (NAACP) is formed.

London hairdressers give the first perms.

Lincoln appears on the penny for the first time.

Rationing
Remember a wartime necessity

Peggy used color copies of her grandmother's ration book to document an important time in American history. Scan and print color copies of pages of ration book and strips of ration stamps; mat on blue cardstock and mount on patterned background paper (NRN Designs). Scan and enlarge page of ration book for journaling paper. Print journaling; mat on blue cardstock. Find posters on the Internet; print out and mat on blue cardstock.

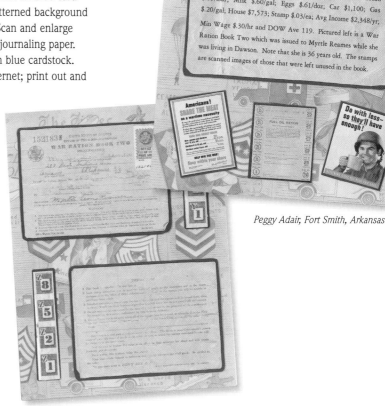

Peggy Adair, Fort Smith, Arkansas

Theresa D. Varela, Albuquerque, New Mexico

A Mother and Her Son Wait Out the War
Demonstrate time passed with age progression

The three pictures represent how much Theresa's Uncle Daniel grew while his father served in WWII. Punch photo mounts (Emagination Crafts), embellishing with a small oval and ⅛" circle punches (Fiskars). Adhere to speckled background (Keeping Memories Alive). For title block, embellish white punched photo mount (Emagination Crafts) using an oval punch and mat with navy. Create title letters (Creating Keepsakes). Color with pencils, punch out with square punch and mat with navy. Adhere to mount and freehand write rest of title. Journal and chalk edges blue.

Kimberly Ling, Fresno, California

Richard Lewis

Use a modern clipping for a heritage layout

If you don't have a vintage clipping for your heritage scrapbook, keep an eye out for "This Day in History" sections in your local newspaper. Kimberly found the perfect clipping fifty years after the event. Trim edge of photo with deckle scissors; double mat on tan and burgundy cardstock. Silhouette crop patch from patterned background paper (NRN Designs) and mount over photo. Write title with brown pen on white cardstock. Double mat title and newspaper clipping with tan and burgundy cardstock.

Cheri O'Donnell, Orange, California

U.S. Navy 1944-45

Honor a woman in wartime

Cheri created this spread for her daughters to remind them of womens' contributions to World War II. For right page, mat portrait on handmade paper; mount on patterned background paper (NRN Designs). Adhere sticker letters (Creative Memories) and write journaling. For page below, mat patterned paper (Paper Patch) on blue background paper. Adhere newspaper clipping and color copies of identification cards. Trim edges of photocopies with decorative scissors.
Adhere military stickers (Creative Memories).
Finish by journaling in blue ink.

The fastest automobile speed ever is recorded: 133 miles per hour.

U.S. population: 91.9 million

Father's Day is celebrated for the first time.

Electric washing machines are available for the first time.

Joseph Pulitzer's will establishes the Pulitzer Prize.

Willis Haviland Carrier invents the air conditioner. Oreos hit the market.

Roald Amundsen's expedition reaches the South Pole.

The Titanic sinks; 1,513 people die.

George Bernard Shaw writes *Pygmalion*, the inspiration behind the musical *My Fair Lady*.

Life magazine lists the slang expressions of the year: flossy, beat it, peeved, fussed.

Peter Joseph Turonski
Scan medals and government documents

Shelley wanted to document her grandfather's WWII service "with pride," she says. For side borders, adhere 2¾" strips of red cardstock. Center 1¼" strip of white on each. Apply punched red maple leaves (Emagination Crafts). Scan (or color copy) medals and discharge document and mat. Double mat photo. Print Canadian flags (Printmaster Platinum 12 by Broderbund), and double mat. Adhere to mat's corners. Print title; mat with red and apply punched leaves.

Shelley McLennan, St. Catherines, Ontario, Canada

Obtaining Government/Vital Records

To re-create an accurate portrayal of someone's life, you'll need documentation—and lots of it. The trick is knowing where to find it and—most important—how to get your hands on it.

A great place to start is your local library, where you'll find a myriad of resources including newspapers, genealogy CD-ROMs, and copies of birth and death certificates. Most libraries also have a genealogical section filled with knowledgeable librarians who are eager to help you search.

As well, you can contact the archival section of the county courthouse in the states in which your ancestors lived. Send them a self-addressed, stamped envelope, along with a detailed letter explaining why you're requesting the documents. In order to obtain the best, most comprehensive results, be sure to include all known information regarding your ancestors, such as birth dates, addresses and maiden names. Be forewarned that many government agencies require the use of a specific form and charge a small fee for copying, so an initial phone call to the archivist to verify these details can help speed up the process.

Once you've exhausted local resources, move on to the federal government's National Archives and Records Administration office, repeating the same process.

Robert W. Seebers

Pay tribute to a family hero

Trina never met her Uncle Bob, but making a scrapbook about his life connected her to him in a tangible way. For the right page, stamp Liberty Collage stamp (Paper Inspirations) on brown cardstock; tear corners and mount over patterned background paper (source unknown). Adhere border stickers (Anna Griffin). Double mat photo with photo corners (K & Co.) on patterned paper (Magenta) and corrugated mustard cardstock (DMD). Print out journaling on ivory cardstock; cut with deckle scissors and chalk edges. Print out title with scanned photos; mat on patterned paper (Anna Griffin). For left page, enlarge and print collage of accident report and photo. Double mat plane photo with purple cardstock and deckle-cut black cardstock. Print poem and copy of letter; tear, chalk and adhere to corners. Create envelope with template (Printworks) from patterned paper (Carolee's Creations). Create "wax seal" with red cardstock, chalk and black and white opaque pens. Write journaling with brown pen. Reduce and print color copies of accident report and sermon; place in envelope.

Trina E. Craig, Duvall, Washington

Now Thank We All Our God

Document a thankful reunion

Paula used pages from a hymnal and a homemade stamp to illustrate her father's joyful homecoming. Mat rust cardstock on patterned paper (Scrapbook Times), leaving a thin border. Copy hymnal page onto glossy cardstock; cover with tan vellum. Single and double mat photos on blue metallic paper (Making Memories) and blue and navy cardstock. Print out journaling; deckle-cut edge and mat on navy cardstock. Adhere border stickers (Mrs. Grossman's) and buttons (LaMode for Concord House). Cut stamp from patterned paper (Scrapbook Times) with stamp edgers (Fiskars); mat on tan cardstock. Finish with hand-drawn postmark.

Paula Buermele, Canton, Michigan

1913

The Sixteenth Amendment grants Congress the right to collect income tax.

First liquor laws are passed.

The Ford Motor Company adopts the assembly line in its automobile plants.

1914

Austrian Archduke Francis Ferdinand and his wife are assassinated, precipitating World War I.

Color movies are made.

The first modern "brassiere" is patented.

1915

Congress establishes the U.S. Coast Guard.

The Fox Film Company is founded, eventually becoming Twentieth Century Fox.

Taxis appear on America's roadways.

Margaret Sanger is arrested for publishing the pro-birth control *Family Limitation*.

At Sea and On Shore
Journal by numbers

This layout memorializes Linda's father's eight years in the military. Her photo border and innovative journaling technique allowed her to fit 24 photos on one spread while still providing brief, yet detailed, journaling. Line edges of 12 x 15" white cardstock with 2½" thick blue border. Crop and mat photos, trimming cream mats with deckle scissors. Adhere border photos in desired sequence and sequentially number those that will correspond to the journaling counterclockwise. Angle remaining matted photos inside border. Print captions, trim with deckle scissors and mat. Print journaling, numbering details as they correspond to the border photos, trim with deckle scissors and double mat. Print title, trim with deckle scissors and double mat. Freehand-cut anchor embellishment. Color copy campaign bar, silhouette and adhere. Adhere military charms.

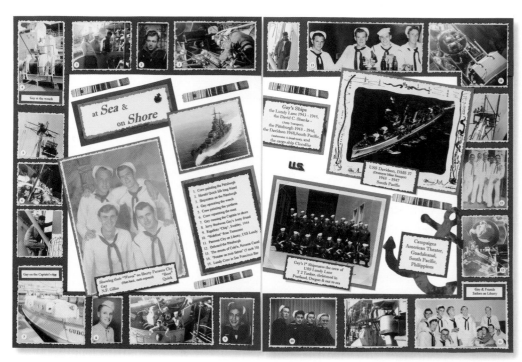

Linda Arnold Milligan, El Paso, Texas

My Sweet P-47
Showcase a special cartoon

Jacqueline created a special tribute to her husband's "first love"—his P-47 plane. Mat photos on cloud patterned paper. Enlarge cartoon and circle-cut. Cut light blue cardstock triangle and adhere to corner. Add title letter stickers (Creative Memories). Cut heart from red cardstock. Finish with journaling in black pen and captions in silver pen.

Jacqueline Querns, Mesa, Arizona

The Brave Go Forth
"Paper tole" dimensional stars that curl

Brandi silhouetted stars from a second piece of the patterned paper used for the background (K & Co.). Curl by placing stars facedown on a soft surface, such as a mouse pad or craft foam. Using an embossing stylus, rub around the star's edges and center. Mount on background with self-adhesive foam spacers. Triple mat photos. Print journaling on clear vellum. Mat with star-patterned paper. Replicate the 1st Cavalry Division emblem from an image downloaded from the Internet. Mount emblem and journaling on navy paper. Print on cardstock and silhouette with a craft knife.

Brandi Ginn, Lafayette, Colorado
Photos: Amy Partain, Colorado Springs, Colorado

Welcome Home
Show the stars and stripes forever

Accurately documenting Company E's return home during WWI required a thoroughly patriotic layout. For background, adhere patterned paper (K & Co.) to torn blue and red paper with nailheads (JewelCraft). Adhere to khaki background. Double mat photos with blue and red. Tear bottom edge of one blue mat and apply star nailheads. Detail mats with gold gel pen. Print journaling on vellum. Cut title letters from template (Scrap Pagerz) and shadow. Detail with gold gel pen.

Jodi Amidei, Lafayette, Colorado

1916

1917

Durst
A military man

Linda found the quilt pattern for this military man in a library book. The paper doll represents her father, who, in this picture, was stationed in the Phillipine Islands during the Korean War. Use a black pen to detail border of cream paper. Angle an 8½ x 11" piece of sage paper for background, trimming edges where needed. Cut doll pieces from pattern (source unknown); adhere to background. Quadruple mat photo with cream paper and brown shades of paper used for doll. Use lettering template (Frances Meyer) for title and mat. Detail and journal with black pen.

Linda Strauss, Provo, Utah

From a Boy to a Man
Achieve military look with dog tags

Holly wanted a basic look for this page to describe her father's tour in Vietnam. Mat photo with black and adhere to blue background. Print title words, name and journaling and mat each. Punch tiny holes near top and bottom of page to secure chain ends with string. Adhere dog tags with self-adhesive foam spacers. Adhere matted title words within chain title.

Holly VanDyne, Mansfield, Ohio

Called to Serve
Create a faux watermark

For the title's background, Brandi downloaded the flag
image from the Internet and recolored it gray to resemble a
watermark. Print title. Mat with red and adhere to background paper (Making Memories). Triple mat photo with
French Lace paper (Making Memories), white and Tommy's
Toys Red Linen Paper (K & Co.). Print journaling on gray
paper. Color copy memorabilia and silhouette to embellish
page. For border, punch white stars (Emagination Crafts).
Use self-adhesive foam spacers to adhere to red strip.
Apply blue fiber (On the Surface).

Brandi Ginn, Lafayette, Colorado

Don Earl Zirkle
Preserve a patriotic portrait

Shirley's color choice lends a patriotic feel to this military
portrait. Print journaling on white cardstock. Mat journaling
and portrait on red cardstock; mount on blue background.
Stamp anchors (PSX Design) and photo corners (Posh
Impressions) on red cardstock. Sprinkle with gold embossing powder and heat-emboss. Silhouette-cut corners and
mount on photo. Cut squares around anchors and mat on
white cardstock.

Shirley Zirkle, Austin, Texas

1918

Russian revolutionaries execute former Czar Nicholas II, his wife and their five children. A rumor circulates that one daughter, Anastasia, survived.

In November, Germany signs the armistice, ending the combat of WWI.

The United States is divided into four time zones. Daylight savings time is initiated.

A year long worldwide influenza epidemic begins, killing 20 million people.

1919

The Eighteenth Amendment prohibits the manufacture and sale of alcohol.

Benito Mussolini founds a fascist political party in Italy.

United Artists Corporation and Radio Corporation of America are formed.

The Julliard School of Music is established.

American baseball fans are horrified by the "Black Sox" bribery scandal.

Jack Dempsey becomes the world heavyweight boxing champion.

Freedom's Price
Tell a story with collage

The collage-like technique on the right side of the layout allowed Pennie to show her pastor's yearlong tour in Vietnam. Readers get to know the young soldier, his friends, interesting scenes, his location and more with her use of photos, a color-copied map and journaling. Trim gray background paper ¾" and mat with blue paper, leaving a ½" border at the top. Embellish top with border stickers (Mrs. Grossman's). Print title. Adhere group photo to left side. Adhere individual photos to right side. Print journaling and mat with red paper (Carolee's Creations). Cut red paper (Carolee's Creations) in banner designs; detail with gold gel pen and adhere around photos. Apply punched white stars (Emagination Crafts). Freehand-cut rifle and combat helmet. Add bits of red paper to bottom of helmet. Wrap wire around helmet in crisscross design. Adhere to background with self-adhesive foam spacers.

Pennie Stutzman, Broomfield, Colorado
Photos: Greg Thompson, Westminster, Colorado

1961 Vietnam

Paper-tear a combat scene

Deborah accented combat photos from Vietnam with military stickers (Frances Meyer) in order to act out a combat scene. Cut border from camouflage patterned paper (Hot Off The Press). Tear brown cardstock for landscape. Mat photos with black cardstock cut with deckle scissors. Cut title letters with lettering template. Finish with military stickers on paper-torn landscape.

Deborah Merghart, La Mesa, California

Vietnam

Paper-piece a combat boot

Stephanie says she did not design this combat-boot paper-piecing pattern specifically with her father in mind, even though he was indeed drafted right out of high school. She says the combat boot "symbolizes the whole turmoil of the sixties, from Kennedy's assassination right to Vietnam." She pieced it with dark brown, olive green and army green cardstock and detailed the top with a white gel pen. Print journaling and double mat. Double mat photos. Adhere to patterned paper background (Paper Adventures) at angles, overlapping each other slightly. Write title; double mat and adhere. Apply boot.

Stephanie Gilbert, Sanford, Florida

Grandma's Hats

Grandma Hoeflich had a closet that was at least twelve feet along one side of their bedroom and filled with outfits of all colors, although I always think of her in lavender. She loved dressing up and had hats, gloves, and a purse to match each outfit. She especially loved hats!

We were allowed to go into a little closet that was under the eaves in her bedroom and get out old hats and gloves and jewelry to play dress-up with – what fun!

She was very outgoing and loved having her picture taken. One of her favorite things was going to the 10¢ store, browsing all the aisles, talking to the clerks, and going into the photo booth to take pictures of herself – but those photos all seem to have disappeared – there were some wonderful hats in those pictures!

The photo on the left was taken April 1947 in the Hotel Peabody in Memphis, Tennessee. The photos on this page are of Grandma and me.

 Families evolve but individuals within them never seem to stray far from their biological and cultural blueprints. Generational pages are a way of recording the similarities between family members as decades move by. What makes these pages unique is that, rather than focusing on a single event or experience, they illustrate the natural flow of events as each generation takes its turn participating in activities such as school portraits, child-rearing and military service. Generational pages may document how a physical trait such as a turned-up nose or high forehead appears in one generation, skips another and then is magically resurrected decades later in an infant. They may also illustrate the growth of a single individual over the course of years. Generational pages remind us of the continuity of life, how we are a link in a chain that connects us to both our ancestors and our offspring.

The Nineteenth
Amendment grants U.S.
women the right to vote.

Grand jury indicts 8 members
of the Chicago White Sox for
fixing the World Series.

Hugh Lofting publishes the
first of the *Dr. Doolittle*
series.

Controversy breaks out
over a new women's fash-
ion—knee-length skirts.

Two physicians test the use
of insulin on dogs with
diabetes.

DeWitt Wallace founds
Reader's Digest.

Philo T. Farnsworth, 15,
develops the idea for a
vacuum tube that makes
television possible.

Supreme court declares
federal child labor law
unconstitutional.

Approximately one out of
every six U.S. marriages
ends in divorce.

Thru the Years

Show family history through fashion trends

Susan used fashion trends as a vehicle to document her female heritage. Each photo frame corresponds to the photo's place in time. For the flower-power frame she used punched flowers and heart and peace-sign stickers (Creative Imaginations). Mat the next photos with white mulberry paper, a cutwork frame (Gina Bear) and flag paper (Hot Off The Press). Print journaling blocks on clear vellum and mat. Mount on black background. Freehand title with white gel pen.

Susan Neill, Shippensburg, Pennsylvania

A History of Military Service

Salute family members in the service

Annalia tied several pictures together with a patriotic military service page. Cut border from patterned paper (Frances Meyer); mount to dark red cardstock. Mat photos with blue cardstock. Write title with opaque white pen on blue cardstock. Finish with journaling in opaque white pen.

Annalia Romero, Silverdale, Washington

Debbie Colomb, Hudson Falls, New York

My Heroes

Trace a valiant family line

The discovery of information about her great-great-grandfathers' service in the Civil War inspired Debbie to honor her brave ancestors. Mat photos with deckle-cut brown cardstock punched with decorative corner punch (All Night Media). Cut 1½ x 12" strips of olive green cardstock; punch with star punch (Family Treasures). Print journaling on patterned paper (Hot Off The Press); cut blocks with deckle scissors and mount. Adhere positive star punch pieces down center of page.

1923

After an unsuccessful rebellion, Adolph Hitler is sent to jail. He writes *Mein Kampf*, his infamous anti-Semitic treatise.

Henry Luce founds *Time* magazine.

President Calvin Coolidge makes the first radio-broadcasted presidential address.

1924

Two women, Nellie Ross in Wyoming and Miriam Ferguson in Texas, are elected governor.

J. Edgar Hoover becomes director of the Federal Bureau of Investigation.

Coach Knute Rockne leads the Notre Dame football team to a perfect season.

1925

Crossword puzzles become extremely popular in the U.S.

London installs the first traffic lights.

Tennessee authorities arrest John Scopes for teaching evolution. He is fined $100.

Michelle Hubbartt, Grand Junction, Colorado

Family Ties With a Swedish Legacy
Capture the feel of a Scandinavian winter

Michelle retraced the steps of a monthlong "road trip" her ancestors took to Sweden in 1923. Mat and triple mat photos with torn and cut silver and gold metallic paper (Club Scrap). Mat largest photo on vellum; mount over torn squares of gold and silver metallic paper accents with punched small snowflakes. Scan and reduce letter; triple mat envelope, leaving top edge of mat open for letter pocket. Print title (Creating Keepsakes) on patterned paper (Club Scrap); color in with gold pen and double mat. Print journaling on vellum; mount to patterned background paper (Club Scrap) with gold eyelets (Creative Impressions). Create right page accents by punching squares from patterned metallic papers; attach large snowflakes (Family Treasures) from metallic papers with gold eyelets. To create left page accent, cut square from patterned paper; double mat with metallic papers. Set small and large gold eyelets; weave white and gold fibers (Club Scrap). Attach eyelets to punched large snowflakes; tie to fibers.

Blest Be the Ties That Bind

Photo transfers for vintage look

By using the photo transfer technique for this page, Julie solved the problem of balancing her contemporary photos with her heritage photos. Follow instructions below to transfer photo images. Next, apply skeletal leaves (All Night Media) to patterned background (Anna Griffin). Connect tags with red ribbon. Knot large ribbon in middle, anchoring tag line by tying small ribbon ends around knots. Cover knots with heart charms (Jesse James). Adhere ribbons and tags to background in flowing design. Apply letter stickers (Mrs. Grossman's) to ribbon. Journal with gold gel pen. Mount background on red cardstock.

Julie K. Eickmeier, Fort Myers, Florida

1. Photocopy photos, enlarging or reducing as needed for intended use. The more contrast there is between light and dark in your photocopy, the better the transfer results will be.

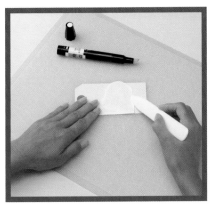

2. Place silhouette-cropped, photocopied image face down onto a cardstock tag. Rub photo transfer AD™ Blender pen (Chartpak) on a small area and then rub firmly but lightly with a bone folder to complete the transfer. Repeat until entire image has been transferred to the tag.

3. Chalk or tint the tags with colored pencils for a distressed look and spray with fixative spray to seal image. Double mat tags.

1926

Ernest Hemingway publishes *The Sun Also Rises*.

A.A. Milne publishes *Winnie-the-Pooh*.

National Broadcasting Company (NBC) is established.

American Gertrude Ederle is the first woman to swim across the English Channel.

The Book-of-the-Month Club is organized and begins signing up members. Some 40,000 join the first year.

You Know Your Dad Loves You When…

Honor generations of fatherly devotion

Memories of her father's love prompted Su to gather photos of fathers and their children throughout her family. Freehand-cut pop-up from patterned paper (Scrap Ease) and adhere to pages. Oval-cut, silhouette-cut or shape-crop photos and mat with ivory cardstock or patterned paper. Trim mats with decorative scissors (Fiskars) and detail with cranberry pen. Mount matted photos over pieces of leaf design (Gina Bear, Scherenschnitte Ltd.) cut from ivory cardstock. Decorate with matted heart stickers. Freehand-cut heart for title and write title in cranberry pen. Finish with journaling in cranberry and white opaque pens.

Su Harris, North Tonawanda, New York

1927

Joseph Stalin takes control of the Soviet Union.

Virginia Woolf publishes *To the Lighthouse*.

Charles Lindbergh pilots the first solo flight across the Atlantic Ocean.

Pavlov publishes the results of his famous conditioned reflex experiments.

Duke Elllington organizes a band and begins to perform at Harlem's Cotton Club.

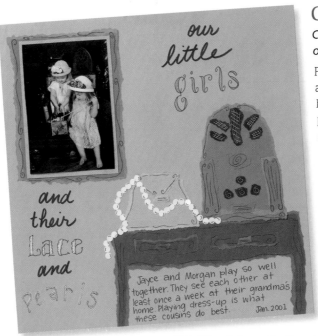

Holle Wiktorek, Fayetteville, Kentucky

Our Little Girls

Capture dress-up in old-fashioned clothing

Photos of children dressing in vintage apparel connect their present to their heritage. Mat photo on parchment paper; mat again on torn brown cardstock. Tear dresser and drawers from mahogany cardstock, radio parts and dresser handles from brown cardstock, purse from tan cardstock and radio knobs from black cardstock. Punch ¼" circles for pearls. Assemble furniture and add pen detailing. Finish with title and journaling.

Great Dads Get Promoted to Grand Dads

Go brown for masculine layout

This simple layout works perfectly for a masculine theme. Use deckle scissors to trim 10" square of patterned paper (NRN Designs). Mount on brown cardstock. Crop and mat photos, trimming left-side mats and right-side black-and-white photos with deckle scissors. For wagon embellishment, cut brown rectangle and punch two 1¼" black circles for tires. Apply sticker (Provo Craft) and detail with black marker and white gel pen. Freehand captions and title, detail borders and frames with white and black gel pens.

Michelle Gowan, Macon, Georgia

Mickey Mouse makes his screen debut in the animated short *Plane Crazy*.

The *New York Times* puts up the first moving electric sign in the U.S. Not surprisingly, the sign goes up in Times Square.

Alexander Fleming discovers penicillin.

October 28 the U.S. Stock Exchange collapses. The Great Depression begins.

Hollywood honors its own at the first Academy Awards.

Ernst Alexanderson uses radio waves to measure an airplane's altitude, paving the way for radar.

The Nazi party becomes the majority party in the German government.

Clyde W. Tombaugh discovers Pluto.

U.S. population is 122.7 million; life expectancy is 61 years. One of every five Americans owns an automobile.

Generations of Special Women
Chronicle matriarchal history

These four pages describe the lives of the women in Linda's family, from her grandmother to her daughter. She used the same layout for each page to symbolize an "inherited energy." Dry emboss floral vine (American Traditional) along one side of pink parchment cardstock (Patchwork Memories). Apply heritage gold and tint border stickers (Me & My Big Ideas) next to embossed border. Quadruple mat large portraits with antique gold cardstock, floral vellum, trimmed with Victorian scissors (Emagination Crafts), burgundy brocade papers (Hot Off The Press) and burgundy cardstock. Oval crop smaller photos and double mat. Apply punched flower embellishments. Freehand journal names on whisper lace nameplates (Mrs. Grossman's) and mat. Print journaling on patterned paper (Paper Cuts), double mat with clear vellum trimmed with deckle scissors and burgundy cardstock. Stamp floral letters (Rubber Stampede), heat emboss with gold embossing powder and double mat. Color with watercolor pencils and markers.

Family Heirloom

Keep focus on story with simple layout

This baby dress has been passed down through three generations in Katy's family. Apply corner stickers (Frances Meyer, Mrs. Grossman's). Mat photos with patterned paper (Making Memories). Print journaling and mat. Embellish title mat with Victorian corner punch (Fiskars). Print title and crop large enough to cover slits made by corner punch. Mat.

Family Heirloom

Here I am in my Christening gown having a ball at the photographers! My mama wore this gown when she was baptized and great grandmother Kathryne Ward Green wore it as a Sunday baby dress. It has been passed down through four generations. I hope that my children will someday wear it as well. It has an over dress and a slip and is made of cotton batiste. My Amma put in green ribbons in the eyelet trim. It dates from around 1904. I love our family traditions.

Katy Danckaert, Annapolis, Maryland

Helen Har Lew Eng Lee was born on September 23, 1929 in Norfolk, Virginia in the United States. She went back to China with her family when she was seven years old. She attended school and grew up in China. Mom married my father (Chiang Wah Lee ※ Bob Lee) in 1948 through an arranged marriage in China. At this time, arranged marriages allowed the prospective bride to refuse the prospective groom after the initial meeting of the two families involved. Shortly after the wedding, my parents sold whatever they owned (most of my Mom's dowery) to get boat passage to America, thus avoiding the uprise of Communism in China.

My parents established a Chinese Hand Laundry business in Chicago, Illinois. Mom has five children: Linda (Me), Sandra, Tony, Evelyn and Salena. After living on the south side of Chicago for eight years, the neighborhood started to change. Unfortunately, the change was not a positive one.

In 1958, my parents relocated the family to New York City to start a new business and a better life. My Mom's motto is "Get a good education and make a better life for yourself than we (meaning our parents) did." Mom had always supported Dad in his plans to make a better life for the family. She was always head strong enough to discuss her own ideas with Dad. Therefore, plans between my parents were never one sided.

In New York, my parents tried working in the restaurant business with partners. That didn't work out. They finally owned Quong Wah Sportswear, Inc. until they retired during the early 1990's. They have four grandchildren: Eugene, Alya Krista, Diana and Matthew. During my parents' golden years, they enjoy visiting the grandchildren and watching them grow. My parents' favorite past time is going on trips around the United States and abroad (China). They also spend a couple of months in Florida staying in their condominium in Del Rey.

Mom is always the one to keep harmony in the family. While my siblings and I were in our teen years, Mom would always take the time to listen to us but she didn't always agree with us. As a young girl, my Mom would always let me stand along beside her and helped while she cooked. She is a fantastic seamstress and she taught me how to make my own clothes. Mom also taught me how to create my own patterns, knit, crochet, string beads, cook and not being afraid to stand up for what I believe in. Mom, just like my grandma, is always an energetic person and on the move constantly.

Linda Weisholz, Putnam Valley, New York

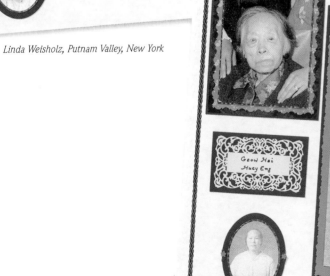

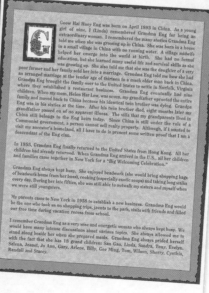

Geow Hai Huey Eng was born on April 1893 in China. As a young girl of nine, I (Linda) remembered Grandma Eng for being an extraordinary woman. I remembered the many stories Grandma Eng told me when she was growing up in China. She was born in a house in a small village in China with no running water. A village midwife helped her emerge into the world at birth. She had no formal education, but she learned many useful life and survival skills as she was growing up. She also told me that she was the daughter of a very poor farmer and her family sold her into a marriage. Grandma Eng told me how she had an arranged marriage at the tender age of thirteen to a much older man back in China. Grandpa Eng brought the family over to the United States to settle in Norfolk, Virginia where they established a restaurant business. Grandma Eng eventually had nine children. When my mom, Helen Har Lew, was seven, my grandfather uprooted the entire family and moved back to China because his identical twin brother was dying. Grandpa Eng was in his sixties at the time. After his twin brother died, eight months later my grandfather passed on of no apparent illness. The villa that my grandparents lived in China still belongs to the Eng heirs today. Since China is still under the rule of a Communist government, a person cannot sell realty property. Although, if I wanted to visit my ancestor's homeland, all I have to do is present some written proof that I am a descendant of the Eng clan.

In 1955, Grandma Eng finally returned to the United States from Hong Kong. All her children had already returned. When Grandma Eng arrived in the U.S., all her children and families came together in New York for a "Big Welcoming Celebration."

Grandma Eng always kept busy. She enjoyed beadwork (she would bring shopping bags of beadwork home from her boss), cooking (especially exotic soups) and taking long walks every day. During her late fifties, she was still able to outwalk my sisters and myself when we were still youngsters.

My parents came to New York in 1958 to establish a new business. Grandma Eng would be the one who took us on shopping trips, jaunts to the park, visits with friends and filled our free time during vacation recess from school.

I remember Grandma Eng as a very wise and energetic woman who always kept busy. We would have many intense discussions about various topics. She always allowed me to stand along beside her when she prepared meals. Grandma Eng always prided herself with the fact that she has 18 grand children: San Gan, Linda, Sandra, Tony, Evelyn, Salena, Jeanet, Jo Ann, Gary, Arlene, Billy, Gee Ming, Tom, Wilson, Sherry, Cynthia, Randall and Stacey.

1931

1932

Vera
Color in mock needlepoint

Shawnna found an easy way to give her pages a homespun look. Double mat photos and journaling blocks with brown and ivory cardstock. Cut a piece of five mesh plastic canvas (available at craft stores) to fit a 12 x 12" page. Align mesh and color in squares of mesh with gold pen to create borders and title. Finish with journaling in gold pen.

Shawnna Gee, Lake Elsinore, California

Family Chain
Link the members of a large family

With more than 50 cousins, Monica struggled with a way to show how her grandparents' family has grown. Her inventive chain shows the connections between her grandparents, their 12 children, more than 50 grandchildren and close to 100 great-grandchildren. Mount paper doilies on patterned background paper (Frances Meyer). Cut 10 x 9" rectangles of burgundy velvet paper (Paper Adventures); frame with strips of brown cardstock. Mount folded doily; double mat recent photo with gold metallic paper (Daler-Rowney-Canford Paper) and white cardstock. Print journaling on white cardstock; mat with gold metallic paper. Oval-cut heritage photo and mat with gold metallic paper. Construct locket cover with gold metallic ovals; trace rubber stamp (PSX Design) over light box with black pen for monogram initial. Oval-cut links of chain and cut "charms" with shape template (Provo Craft) from gold metallic paper. Punch holes in charms and string to chain with gold metallic thread. Finish with names in black ink on links.

Monica Sautter, Greenwood, South Carolina

His Folks, Her Folks

Juxtapose the past with the present

Giving precedence to the black-and-white photos gave Kari's own wedding photos a more romantic touch. Trim photos with deckle scissors and double mat. Freehand journal and title. Apply wedding stickers (Frances Meyer).

a touch of the past ~ a piece of cake ~ a touch of the past ~ a piece of cake ~

His Folks

Lawrence and Janice Murphy 1962

a touch of the past ~ a piece of cake ~ a touch of the past ~ a piece of cake ~

Her Folks

Dean and Irina Davis 1957

Kari Murphy, Olympia, Washington

Prohibition ends with the ratification of the Twenty-first Amendment.

Mae West delivers her famous line "Come up and see me sometime" in the film *She Done Him Wrong*.

The Chicago Bears beat the New York Giants in the first National Professional Football League Championship.

1934

Adolf Hitler names himself Führer of Germany.

Benny Goodman organizes one of the first swing bands.

Dust storms that blow the topsoil from the Great Plains force farmers to abandon their farms and head to California.

1935

The Nuremberg laws exclude Jews from German civic rights.

Congress establishes Social Security.

The beer can is introduced in New Jersey.

Home Grown
Show how a garden grows

A 20-year gap in Briana's photos show how her father—and his impressive garden—have changed. Mat photos on green cardstock and mount to patterned background paper (Provo Craft). Print journaling on white cardstock; double mat on brown and green cardstock. Cut block and tear signpost from brown cardstock. Mat block on paper-torn green cardstock; adhere sticker letters (EK Success). Tear grass; punch flowers and swirls (both EK Success) and mount to base of signpost. Tear title blocks; chalk edges and layer with vegetable cutouts (Handmade Scraps). Cut title letters with lettering template (EK Success). Mat "grown" with torn burgundy cardstock; detail "home" with white opaque pen.

Briana Fisher, Milford, Michigan

Signs of the Times

Preserve handwriting samples

Match photos with signatures to capture a changing personality. Cut three 2 x 12" strips from green patterned paper; accent with arches cut from pink vellum and mount to patterned background paper (Sandylion). Use transfer paper or a light box to copy handwriting onto light green patterned paper; trace over writing with pink marker. Mat photos with pink patterned paper (Karen Foster Design). Cut border from pink patterned paper and corner accents from floral patterned paper (Anna Griffin). Cut title from green cardstock; mat with green patterned paper. Tie buttons with pink string and adhere to corners. Finish with journaling in green pen.

Photos Dawn Mabe, Lakewood, Colorado
Art Pamela Frye, Denver, Colorado

Documenting Genealogical Records

Documentation is the key component to a successful and credible family tree. Although you may choose to be more detailed, at a bare minimum, it is essential to include the following information: where and when you found the record, the type of record you researched, as well as the author, title and page number of the source.

Everybody has a unique method of documentation, but regardless of how you choose to approach it, always remember this one hard and fast rule: Record enough information so that another researcher can determine what and where you have searched!

A standard Pedigree Worksheet, which is similar to the family trees you drew back in grade school, can be found for free on most genealogy Web sites. An inexpensive writer's style guide, such as the *MLA Handbook*, which details the mechanics of writing, such as punctuation, quotation and documentation of sources, can help with virtually every citation question you have.

Remember, genealogy demands precision and consistency, so don't get too creative. It's a time-consuming process, but if you ever need to refer back to a specific fact or re-look something up, you'll be grateful for all your hard work.

1936

Adolf Hitler and Benito Mussolini form the Rome-Berlin axis.

Margaret Mitchell publishes *Gone With the Wind*.

African-American athlete Jesse Owens wins four gold medals at the Berlin Olympics. Hitler had claimed that the Aryan Germans would dominate.

1937

Walt Disney's *Snow White and the Seven Dwarfs* becomes the first feature-length animated film.

The largest German airship ever, the Hindenburg, explodes in Lakehurst, N.J.

Amelia Earhart's plane disappears over the Pacific Ocean.

1938

Orson Welles broadcasts the radio play *Invasion From Mars*, causing a widespread panic when people mistake it for a news broadcast.

Congress creates the House Committee on Un-American Activities, which will lead the Communist witch hunt during the McCarthy era.

Five Generations of Young Women
Add dimension with patterned paper

This layered background technique looks great and is easy to create. Double mat photos with rose cardstock and purple patterned paper (Making Memories) and adhere to background (K & Co.) Use two more pieces of the background paper to silhouette crop images and adhere over their corresponding images with self-adhesive foam spacers. Journal on rose cardstock with gold gel pen.

Erikia Ghumm, Brighton, Colorado

Robert and Maxine

Draw a cross-stitch pattern

Florence created the look of a cross-stitch sampler without sewing one bit. Create border, title blocks and frame using the steps below. Then double mat photo on green and burgundy cardstock with black photo corners.

Florence Davis, Winter Haven, Florida

1. Choose a cross-stitch pattern. Starting at a corner, count the spaces filled by the design. Count the same number of spaces on 14-count perforated paper (available at craft stores); mark the number of perforated spaces needed to re-create the design.

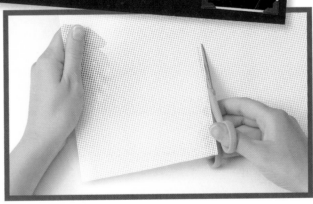

2. Cut the paper, basing your cut lines on the number of spaces previously determined necessary. If you're tentative about cutting the paper, you may proceed to step #3 and cut out the paper later, after your design is complete.

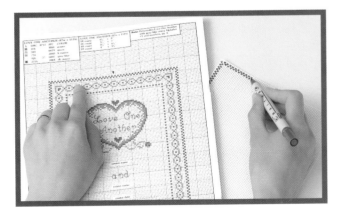

3. Beginning at an outside edge. Working around the border of the pattern, firmly press the point of a 1.2 mm pen into each paper space that coordinates with the cross-stitch pattern's design. Each dot is equal to a single stitch. For thicker stitches use a fine-tipped pen.

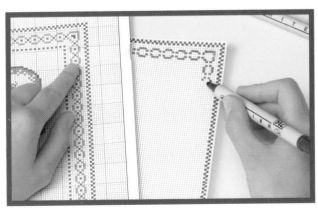

4. Once you've finished filling in the pattern's outer edges, proceed in the same way until you've filled in the rest of the design.

Victor Fleming directs *Gone With the Wind*. Hattie McDaniel becomes the first African-American to win an Oscar for her role in the film.

Irving Berlin's "God Bless America" hits the air-waves.

Germany invades Poland, prompting Britain and France to declare war. World War II begins.

The new film *The Wizard of Oz* entrances American audiences.

1940

Germany invades Denmark, Norway, Belgium, The Netherlands, Luxembourg and France.

U.S. population: 131.6 million. U.S. life expectancy: 63 years

Ernest Hemingway publishes *For Whom the Bell Tolls*.

The Fair Labor Standards Act takes effect, standardizing the 40-hour work week.

The U.S. Congress creates the Selective Service System, requiring all men between the ages of 21 and 36 to register for military service.

The Cars
Document a love affair with the American automobile

Photos of her father-in-law with his cars inspired Sandra to capture the evolving styles of American vehicles. Trim edges of photos with antique scissors (Creative Memories). Mat on trimmed blue and pink cardstock; mount on patterned background paper. Cut blocks for title; write one letter in each block. Line edge of title blocks with green marker. Finish with journaling in black ink.

Sandra Van Heusden, St. Clair Shores, Michigan

Career Soldier
Create a "Then and Now" page

This layout shows Sherry's husband at the time of his army induction in 1978 with his 1998 retirement photo. This is the first page in his military retirement album. For border, decorate strip of gold paper (Canson) with stars cut from camouflage paper (Design Originals) and matted with black. Mat photos. Freehand design red beret, adding color-copied service badge. Journal with black pen, matting with red. Trim mat with Heartbeat scissors (Fiskars). Add year captions.

Sherry Grant, Fuquay-Varina, North Carolina

The Lester Farm
Remember a cherished family home

Kathryn recorded her fond memories of her grandparents' farm in an elegant scrapbook page. Mount patterned paper (Hot Off The Press) at an angle on maroon cardstock; trim corners at edges of cardstock. Print journaling and caption on cream cardstock. Mat photos and caption on tan cardstock; mat journaling on brown cardstock.

Kathryn Frolian, Columbus, Ohio

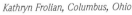

In the Spring…
Illustrate an unusual family tradition

The moment she saw her father wearing a dress, Emily knew the event was destined for a scrapbook page. Stamp feathers (Uptown Design Company) on purple cardstock. Create border by sprinkling adhesive tape with black embossing powder and heating. Double mat photos with gold photo corners (Canson) on purple cardstock and blue velvet paper (Wintech). Write journaling in gold opaque pen; mat name and year with blue velvet paper. Write title in black and gold pen; mount to page with gold photo corners. Stamp additional feather and silhouette crop cut for accent.

Emily Zimmer, Spanish Fork, Utah

1941

Mount Rushmore is finished.

Orson Welles directs and stars in *Citizen Kane*.

The Manhattan Project begins its research on the atomic bomb.

Lou Gehrig, one of America's most beloved baseball players, dies.

On December 17, Japanese forces launch a surprise attack on the U.S. base at Pearl Harbor. The United States enters World War II.

1942

Nazi soldiers begin using gas chambers to enforce Hitler's "Final Solution." Before the war is over, six million Jews will die in German death camps.

Irving Berlin writes the song "White Christmas."

The U.S. government forces 100,000 Japanese-Americans into internment camps.

U.S. naval forces undermine Japanese naval superiority at the Battle of Midway.

The jitterbug is the dance of the times.

John Turner Littell
Photograph large family heirlooms

Photographs can preserve the memory of heirlooms that are too big or bulky to include in a scrapbook. Cut an 8½ x 11" piece of cream cardstock in half width-wise; mount over top half of tan cardstock. Cut black cardstock in half lengthwise; mount on right side of tan cardstock. Decorate background with stickers (Me and My Big ideas). Mat chair photos on black cardstock. Mat portrait on white cardstock with tan photo corners (Hero Arts). Print journaling on white cardstock; mat on black cardstock with corner stickers (Me and My Big ideas). Print name-plate on white cardstock, decorate with stickers, and mat on ivory cardstock with photo corners.

Tammy Lutz, High Point, North Carolina

Two Mexican Vacations

Contrast two generations

When Victoria dropped off her daughter and her daughter's friends at the airport for their trip to Cancun, it reminded her of her own Mexican vacation that she took with her college friends in 1968. While taking pictures, she suddenly realized how times have changed—today's generation of young women seem a little more relaxed. Double mat photos and adhere to tropical patterned paper (Wübie). Print title and journaling and mat.

Victoria Severson, Arlington Heights, Illinois

Photographing Memorabilia

A picture of family heirlooms and heritage memorabilia preserves those items in your scrapbook without adding bulk. Try these great tips:

- Outdoors, use 200-speed film and flash; shoot in open shade or soft sunlight.

- Indoors, use 400-speed film and flash; shoot in well-lit location or late in the day for a nostalgic effect.

- Arrange memorabilia on floor or tabletop in an eye-pleasing display.

- Fill the frame with your arrangement.

- Move in as close as possible to better see words and numbers.

- Shoot the same photos or arrangements from different angles. If you like, rearrange materials and reshoot for more options.

- As an alternative for flat memorabilia such as medals and certificates, scan the item(s) into your computer, either alone or as a collage. Reduce the size and print on acid-free paper.

PORTRAITS AND FAMILY TREES

 Portraits, those formal and often staid photos of individuals or groups, say so much about the people in the image. While their expressions may seem to offer little clue as to what is in the subjects' minds or hearts, the setting of the photo speaks volumes.

These less-than-candid pictures capture individuals as they wish to be remembered, decked out in their finery, posed with treasured possessions or beloved animals. Portraits are "best foot forward" photos and scrapbooking them ensures the posterity of the posers. Family trees are a beautiful way of pulling together portraits and illustrating family relationships and lineage. Like families, family trees are constantly evolving, growing and changing. But their bases remain firmly planted, even as the branches extend upward and beyond. Family trees are especially important in our mobile society. It is far too easy to forget our roots when most of us no longer reside down the block from great-grandparents, uncles and cousins. Family trees are a road map with which we can trace our way home. Whether creating a family tree, or featuring a single family member's portrait in your scrapbook, you'll marvel at the individuality of your forebears.

1943

Rodgers and Hammerstein II collaborate to produce *Oklahoma!*.

The U.S. government issues rationing coupon books for certain foods.

A race riot in Harlem kills five, injures over 400 and causes $5 million in damage.

1944

On June 6 (D-Day), Allied troops begin their European invasion at Normandy in France.

At the Battle of the Bulge, Allied forces push the German army back.

President Franklin D. Roosevelt wins an unprecedented fourth term.

1945

The U.S. drops the atomic bomb on the Japanese cities of Hiroshima and Nagasaki. Japan surrenders to the Allies on August 14.

Vice President Harry S. Truman is sworn in after Franklin Roosevelt's death.

The war in Europe ends on May 8.

Traditional Family Tree
Make flaps for extra information

Nancy put a twist on the traditional family tree by including important information beneath each person's photo about his or her life. Scan photos and enlarge to desired size; print out and mat on green cardstock, cutting the cardstock twice as long as photo to allow for flap fold. Fold mat in half and mount bottom side to patterned paper (Provo Craft). Print photo captions and title (Creating Keepsakes) on white cardstock; mat on green cardstock. Print journaling on white cardstock and mount inside each flap.

Nancy Grayheck, Hinsdale, Illinois

Pedigree Chart
Build from youngest to oldest

Laurie created a scrapbook page based on a pedigree chart—a common form used to document family relationships. The youngest member on the chart is placed at the left and ancestor couples extend to the right in the pattern shown below. Reduce and print photos and clip art (Dover Publications) with captions on white acid-free paper; double mat on gray and black cardstock. Mount photos in pedigree arrangement on patterned background paper (NRN Designs). Accent youngest member with crown borders (Family Treasures) punched from green and black cardstock. Punch mega bare trees (Nankong), small birch leaves (Marvy/Uchida) and grass border (McGill) and assemble for tree accent. Cut borders from black cardstock; accent with Victorian corner die cuts. Print title on patterned paper. Triple mat title with gray, green and black cardstock.

Laurie Nelson Capener, Providence, Utah

The first General Assembly of the United Nations meets in London.

The United States grants the Philippines independence.

Winston Churchill delivers his famous "Iron Curtain" speech in Fulton, Mo. Historians consider this the start of the Cold War.

Dr. Benjamin Spock publishes *The Commonsense Book of Baby and Child Care.*

Anne Frank's diary is published.

Wartime draft ends.

Young shepherds discover the Dead Sea Scrolls in a cave in the Judean Desert.

Tennessee Williams publishes *A Streetcar Named Desire.*

Dr. Edwin Land announces his new invention—the Polaroid camera.

Jackie Robinson becomes the first African-American major-league baseball player.

Hourglass Family Tree
Document generations forward and backward

Peggy, along with the help of her husband, Jim, was able to find information and photographs for seven generations of her mother's family. An hourglass format helped her organize the information forward and backward in time. Scan, reduce and print photos; mat on green cardstock printed with name and birth year. Arrange photo in hourglass pattern shown below; mount to patterned background paper (Anna Griffin). Accent main photo and corners of spread with charms (Boutique Trims, Inc.). Connect photos with fibers (On the Surface).

Peggy Adair, Fort Smith, Arkansas

Family Trees for Stepfamilies, Adoptions and Divorces

Are you challenged with incorporating members of your stepfamily into your family tree? Frustrated by secrets family members are holding? Here are some tips to help you with unique situations:

- If you have a stepfamily situation, consider color-coding to indicate which members are "steps" and which are biological descendants. Or make two trees—one with the "step," and the other strictly biological.

- If an individual has been divorced, you can make a simple notation in the tree. Include the ex's ancestry only if there were children from that union.

Fan Family Tree
Include a personal timeline

Laurie documented four generations of ancestors in a fan family tree and included a timeline of her own photos to show how she changed within her own lifetime. Draw fan design following format below. (Laurie drew her tree from a template designed by Tony Matthews of Paper Tree, www.grillyourgranny.com.) Handcut borders from burgundy and white cardstock. Computer print names on white paper; trim and mat on brown cardstock. Scan, reduce and print photographs with captions; mount on burgundy border. Accent fan with punched mini flowers repunched with 1/16" circles, small birch leaves and mini swirls (Marvy/Uchida). Punch title (Family Treasures).

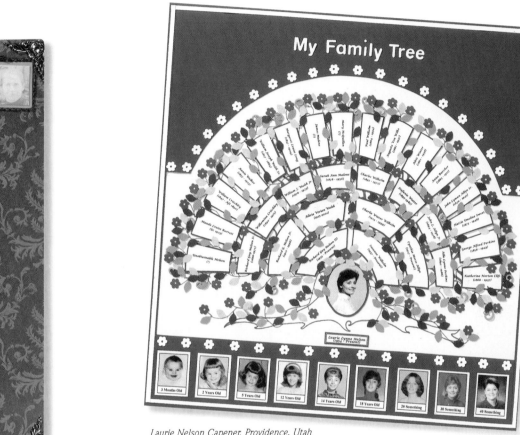

Laurie Nelson Capener, Providence, Utah

- Act likewise for adoptions. If the adopted individual or parents do not want you to research his ancestry, you should honor that request. But note the adoption on your personal family tree so future generations can research their heritage.

- Remember that everything you include should be public information. Including unsubstantiated hearsay in your family tree can be dubious. If you choose to do so, be sure to note your source(s).

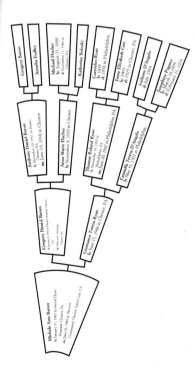

The nation of Israel is established and promptly attacked by surrounding Arab nations.

The Soviet Union blockades West Berlin to force Western nations out, but the U.S. and others airlift supplies into the besieged city.

Eero Saarinen designs the Gateway Arch for St. Louis.

Western nations form the North Atlantic Treaty Organization (NATO).

George Orwell publishes *1984*.

The American Cancer Society and the National Cancer Institute report a possible link between cigarettes and cancer.

North Korea invades South Korea, prompting President Harry Truman to send U.S. troops. The Korean War begins.

Charles Schultz creates Charlie Brown and the Peanuts gang.

Numeric Tracking
Connect a family tree with individual profiles

Jenna assigned each person in her family a number. By documenting the numbers on a family tree, she helps her readers place individual family members in the context of the overall family tree. To create flower family tree, punch medium circles from white cardstock; mat with large circles and super jumbo flowers from patterned papers (Colors by Design). Carefully measure the distance between flowers and connect with freehand-cut stems and leaves. Journal in black pen on circles and on rounded rectangle journaling block. Mat journaling block on black cardstock. Finish with chalk details.

Jenna Beegle, Woodstock, Georgia

Color Coding

Identify individuals with family lines

Jane created a simple color code in her heritage album to indicate whether ancestors were descendants of her mother or her father. Each colored photo mat reflects a specific individual's lineage. To re-create Jane's color system, use mauve cardstock for mother's side and green cardstock for father's side. Mat photos accordingly.

This Album was Compiled by
Jane Amelia Casebolt (nee Taylor)
1998
Color Code
☐ Fathers Side
☐ Mothers Side
☐ Both Sides

Edmond John Christian Leischer

Paternal Grandmother: Jenny (Kreuger) Taylor 1853-1917
Her three children left to right: Pearl, Ora John, and Mae
This picture and prayer

SEE THE ILLUMINATED WATER FALLS OSCEOLA

Jane and John: 1943

Jane and David: 1944

Ready For Church: 1942
Bud, Dick, Dan, Dad, Jane, Dave

Jane and sister, Pat 1942

The Gift Of A Family

Daniel, Bud, Jane, Richard, David 1943

Daddy(Ora John) and Jane: 1944

The Cousins: 1939
Audry Peach, Sally Tiede,
Jane Taylor, Aunt Edna Colene Grieves
Joan Day, Jean Sowers, Janet Ebert

Jane Casebolt, Rocklin, California

1951

The Columbia Broadcasting System (CBS) shows the first commercial color television broadcast.

Scientists in Idaho use nuclear power to produce electricity.

With special glasses, audiences can enjoy 3-D movies.

William Dale Hubbartt
Add color to a sepia layout

A tinted photograph and bright beads add a subtle dash of color to a heritage layout. Double mat tinted photograph on patterned paper (Die Cuts With a View) and brown cardstock with gold photo corners (Canson); mount patterned background paper (Die Cuts With a View). Print title on vellum; attach to mat with brown eyelets (Creative Impressions). Punch six primitive hearts (Emagination Crafts) from brown cardstock; wrap with wire strung with beads. Double mat hearts on patterned paper and cardstock.

Michelle Hubbartt, Grand Junction, Colorado

1952

Queen Elizabeth II of England takes the throne.

The world's first hydrogen bomb is successfully tested.

"Panty raids" are a frequent occurrence on college campuses throughout the nation.

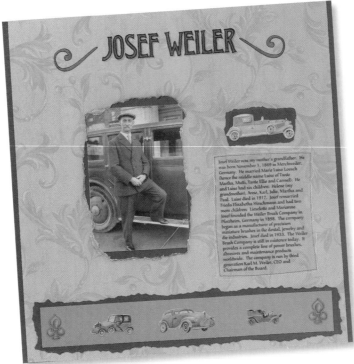

Corina Minkoff,
Cedar Grove, New Jersey

Josef Weiler
Mimic worn photo with torn frame

The distressed edges around the photo lend a vintage look to this layout. Mount photo on burgundy cardstock, just left of center. Tear out hole in patterned paper (K & Co.) just left of center to frame photo. Apply antique car stickers (Provo Craft) and fleur de lis stickers (NRN Designs) to gold strip of paper. Chalk edges of fleur-de-lis stickers. Mat with torn burgundy and adhere to bottom border. Apply single car sticker to torn burgundy block. Print journaling on clear vellum, tear edges and detail with red pen. Print title. Add swirl details using template (C-Thru Ruler). Outline title with black pen and color in with red pencil.

1953

Arthur Miller publishes *The Crucible*. Hugh Hefner founds *Playboy*.

Francis Crick and James Watson propose that the structure of DNA follows a double-helix shape.

Edmund Hillary and Tenzing Norgay are the first people to reach the summit of Mount Everest.

Gertrude Blackwell

Find embellishment ideas in quilting patterns

Jenna found inspiration for her punch art from a quilting design. Mat photo with clay cardstock. Mat block of patterned paper (K & Co.) with white cardstock for frame. Using an oval cutter, remove center. For embellishments, punch green tulips (HyGlo/American Pin) for base. For roses, layer large ash leaf (Punch Bunch) over small waterdrops (EK Success). Make daisies by punching small suns (EK Success) and applying mini daisies from flower corner punch negatives (Fiskars) and ⅛" circles on top. Mount framed photo on golden yellow cardstock. Journal with black pen.

Jenna Beegle, Woodstock, Georgia

Punch multiple small tulip, leaf, water drop, mini daisies, ⅛" circles and sun shapes. Cut and layer as shown on the page above.

William Golding publishes
Lord of the Flies.

Jonas Salk develops his
injectable polio vaccine.

Twenty-six comic book
publishers voluntarily agree
to eliminate vulgar,
obscene and horror comics.

The U.S. Supreme Court rules
that segregation in public
schools is unconstitutional.

Marlon Brando delivers his
Oscar-winning performance
in *On the Waterfront.*

1955

On December 1, Rosa
Parks is arrested in
Montgomery, Ala., for
refusing to give up her bus
seat to a white man. Dr.
Martin Luther King Jr.
organizes a boycott of the
segregated city buses.

Lawrence Welk begins his
weekly variety show.

Jim Henson creates Kermit
the Frog.

Disneyland in Anaheim,
California, opens to visitors.

The U.S. Air Force Academy
opens.

L.O. Powell
Punch and weave a frontier border

Sue pays tribute to a Texas ancestor with rough and rowdy accents. Punch edges of patterned paper (Keeping Memories Alive) with film strip punch (Family Treasures); weave raffia in and out of border, tying off at corners and mid points. Mount patterned paper to black cardstock background. Double mat photo with black and brown cardstock; mount to patterned paper with black photo corners (Fiskars). Write journaling in black ink on brown cardstock; mat with black cardstock. Stamp photo corners (Hero Arts) and mount to corners of journaling block. Finish with punched stars.

Sue Kelemen, St. Louis, Missouri

Katia Clift Perkins and the Rose
Relate a humorous family story

Laurie used rose accents to tie her spread together and to connect her design to her journaling. Print journaling on white cardstock; triple mat journaling and photo with red and pink cardstock. Create borders by punching patterned paper (The Gifted Line) and red and pink cardstock with scallop corner punch (McGill—remove side inserts); layer and mount. Accent border with die-cut vines (Accu-Cut) and oak leaves (Family Treasures) punched from green textured paper (SEI). Add clip art (Dover Publications) and stickers (American Greetings Stickers; The Gifted Line) mounted on self-adhesive foam spacers.

Laurie Nelson Capener, Providence, Utah

Mildred Comstock

Layer papers for a vintage border

Oksanna punched, stamped and used patterned paper to help decorate a beautiful portrait. Computer print journaling. Color in title letters with pink glitter pen. Double mat photo with tan cardstock punched with Victorian corner photo slot punch (Fiskars) and rust cardstock. Mount photo on patterned paper (K & Co.) bordered with strips of rust cardstock. Create border on right page by layering patterned paper cut with Wide Colonial paper edger (Fiskars), cardstock cut with Long Colonial paper edger (Fiskars), tan cardstock punched with ivy border punch (All Night Media), patterned paper, tan cardstock and rust cardstock. Punch ash leaf (Punch Bunch) from green vellum; mount along edges. Stamp chunky maple leaf (Duncan Enterprises) on green vellum; silhouette cut. Finish title with letters cut from rust cardstock with brush letters template (C-Thru). Accent mat and border with gold metallic thread (All Night Media).

Oksanna Pope, Los Gatos, California

Katherine Mae Johns

Scan cloth heirlooms

Christine wanted to display her grandmother's handkerchief on this layout, but it was too big. Her solution? Scan it with the burgundy paper behind it, reduce it and silhouette the image to use behind the matted photo. She also reduced the handwriting on the back of the photo and matted it to use as a corner embellishment. Double mat photo and adhere over handkerchief. Tie black ribbon into bow on heart charm (Darice). Adhere to brown cardstock square, chalk with brown and mat. Print title and journaling on brown cardstock, chalk brown and mat.

Christine J. Holmer, Elmwood Park, Illinois

Elvis Presley's "Heartbreak Hotel" becomes an instant hit.

Autherine Lucy, the first African-American student at the University of Alabama, is suspended after three days of violence. The NAACP takes the university to court.

Charlton Heston stars in Cecil B. DeMille's *The Ten Commandments*.

1957

Dr. Seuss publishes *The Cat in the Hat* and *The Grinch That Stole Christmas*.

10-year-old Robert Strom wins $192,000 on *The $64,000 Question*.

Congress passes the Civil Right Act, prohibiting discrimination.

My Grandma Polly
Include era-appropriate facts and stamps

Elegant color blocking and informative facts put a portrait in perspective. Print journaling; cut out blocks and mount. Freehand-cut blocks of purple and olive cardstock, patterned paper (Hot Off The Press), and gray cardstock blocks for stamping. Arrange blocks to fit page, leaving space to allow black background to show through. Add pre-printed journaling blocks (CKC Creations). Mat photo with embossed frame (Keeping Memories Alive) and patterned paper. Finish with stamped accents (Raindrops on Roses).

Carolyn Hassall, Bradenton, Florida

No Greater Heroine
Accent with origami

Diana created a tribute to her grandmother in Okinawa with Japanese-inspired origami and haiku. Double mat patterned paper (Ever After Scrapbook Co.) with gray and blue cardstock. Double mat photo on printed (Penny Black) and blue vellum. Print journaling on white textured paper (Lasting Impressions). Fold origami crane. Stamp with kanji of family name (custom-made in Japan) and heat-emboss with gold embossing powder.

Diana Bishop, Draper, Utah

Wilma Joyce Gore

Feature yourself on a heritage page

Joyce decide to create a "Me" album, giving her descendants the opportunity to know her as a person. Scan in photos and create photo collage in photo manipulation program; add journaling and print on ivory cardstock. Double mat photo collage on blue and rust textured cardstock (Club Scrap). Print nameplate (Creating Keepsakes); mat with rust cardstock. Stamp border (Leaves of Time).

Time is a dressmaker specializing in alterations.
~ FAITH BALDWIN

daughter
sister....
wife....
mother....
grandmother....
Me!

Wilma Joyce Gore
born August 27, 1946

Joyce Locke, Portales, New Mexico

Using Your Computer for Genealogical Research

Gone are the days of expensive, time-consuming trips to libraries, churches and government offices around the country only to learn that the documents regarding your ancestors aren't even there. Today, with the ever-expanding power of the Internet, genealogy research has never been easier. Today's genealogist simply has to log on to one of the countless genealogy Web sites by typing in key words such as "Ellis Island" and "National Archives and Records Association" or by visiting Web sites like FamilySearch.org. Then, just type in the family name and wait for the computer to find your ancestors. Add to that the many computer programs designed to organize your work, and CD-ROMs bursting with ship manifests and census information, and suddenly, your family tree is in full bloom.

1959

Pope John XXIII calls Vatican Council II, which will radically modernize Catholic dogma and practices.

Alaska and Hawaii become the 49th and 50th states, respectively.

Fidel Castro names himself leader of a totalitarian regime in Cuba.

The Dalai Lama seeks asylum in India after Chinese troops occupy Lhasa, Tibet.

Ethel Merman stars in *Gypsy* and Mary Martin stars in *The Sound of Music*.

1960

Harper Lee publishes *To Kill a Mockingbird.*

In music, Chubby Checker records "The Twist" and Motown Records is founded.

Hitchcock releases the suspense classic *Psycho.*

Jane Goodall begins studying African chimpanzees.

Israeli agents capture German war criminal Adolf Eichmann in Argentina. He is tried and found guilty of crimes against humanity. He is hanged several years later.

Great Aunt Millie Kalsem
Craft a floral border

Linda gave this portrait a feminine touch with the careful combination of coordinating patterned paper. Triple mat photo with patterned papers (Carolee's Creations) and purple cardstock; mount on patterned background paper (K & Co.). Print journaling (Creating Keepsakes) on patterned paper (Carolee's Creations); mat with purple cardstock. Cut floral squares from patterned paper (K & Co.); double mat with decorative squares (Family Treasures) punched from patterned paper and purple cardstock.

Linda Cron, Palm Harbor, Florida

Lauree Sakeida, Honolulu, Hawaii

Jino Hiranaka
Look to cultural artifacts for inspiration

Japanese objects inspired Lauree's color scheme and design elements. Tear the edges of a 12 x 12" sheet of vellum; position diagonally and adhere corners to backside of black cardstock. Accent edges of page with purple ribbon. Print journaling on computer on gray marble paper (source unknown). Punch holes in journaling block and weave in purple ribbon. Double mat photos and journaling with purple and black cardstock. Photocopy family crest; color with black pen and emboss with clear embossing powder. Silhouette crop. Mount on black cardstock. Double mat with vellum and purple cardstock; punch holes and weave ribbon.

Gibson Beck Fullerton

Punch a masculine border

Mary Faith had very little information about her grandfather, but her strong, masculine accents communicate her feelings about him. Mat photo on red cardstock. Punch 1¼" squares from green cardstock, slice in half and adhere to corners. Print journaling on tan cardstock; mat on plaid patterned paper (Colorbök). Print title on tan cardstock; double mat with red cardstock and plaid patterned paper. Create border by cutting a strip of red cardstock and strip of plaid patterned paper with wavy scissors. Cut 3 x 12" strips of red cardstock and plaid patterned paper; adhere to opposite wavy-cut strip. Punch desired size squares from various papers; alternate papers in a line down sides of page and along bottom and top of right page. Top with stickers (Provo Craft) and gold brads.

Mary Faith Roell, Harrison, Ohio

Grandma

Use photo border to accentuate detail

Paula alternated cut squares of White Blossoms Shotz paper (Creative Imaginations) with her own cropped black-and-white photos of blossoms for this border. She has fond memories of picking cherries at her grandmother's house and wanted to bring attention to the cherry blossoms in the photo background. Crop photo and mat with olive paper. Apply clear beads to middle of punched flowers (EK Success) and adhere to corners. Mount photo to background over torn piece of patterned vellum (Colorbök) with olive strip in center. Print journaling on cream paper. Attach to background with gold eyelets in corners. Thread bottom eyelets with fiber. Cut title from Shotz paper and black-and-white photos using lettering template (EK Success). Embellish letters with punched flowers accented with glass beads.

Paula DeReamer, Alexandria, Minnesota

1961

President John F. Kennedy establishes the Peace Corps.

Communists build the Berlin Wall.

Soviet cosmonaut Yuri Gagarin becomes the first man in space. A month later Alan Shepard becomes the first American in space.

1962

Wilt Chamberlain becomes the first professional basketball player to score 100 points in a game.

Johnny Carson takes over as host of "The Tonight Show" from Jack Paar.

John Glenn becomes the first American to orbit the Earth.

1963

The Beatles dominate England's pop charts.

Dr. Martin Luther King Jr. delivers his famous "I Have a Dream" speech.

On November 22, U.S. President John F. Kennedy is assassinated while riding in a motorcade in Dallas.

Louise Trotter
Make a pleated frame

Bay pleated an entire 12 x 12" sheet of patterned paper (Anna Griffin) for this frame. For pleating instructions, see page at right. Sew fibers (Cut-It-Up) and satin ribbon to 8" lavender square that has been matted with clear vellum. Cover stitches with silhouetted flower images from patterned paper (Anna Griffin). Center over pleated frame. Make photo card from folded lavender paper. Line inside of lavender paper with patterned, cream paper (Anna Griffin). Apply photo to outside with clear photo corners. Adhere silhouetted flower images to inside and outside of card. Print journaling on patterned vellum (Anna Griffin). Freehand caption on same vellum. Embellish with more silhouetted flower images. Apply crystal lacquer and glass micro beads to flowers on mat and on corner of photo card.

Bay Loftis, Philadelphia, Tennessee

1. Use a pencil and metal straightedge ruler to draw parallel lines across the back of 12 x 12" patterned paper of choice. Retrace lines with the pointy tip of a bone folder, pressing lightly to score the lines for folding.

2. Use both hands to lightly pinch the scored lines, coaxing the lines up into a peak that can be folded. Fold all drawn and scored lines.

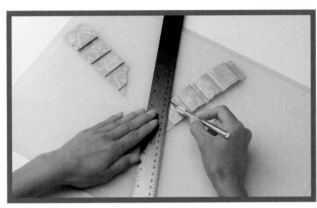

3. Hold all folded pleats flat and place a metal straightedge ruler on top of paper. Use a craft knife to cut the folded page into 1½" strips, slicing down upon the folds and not up against the folds. Fold strip flat to compress it and attach tape adhesive to keep it flat.

4. Use a metal straightedge ruler and craft knife to "miter" corners at a 45-degree angle where border strips meet at page corners; adhere in place.

Quilt Page

Punch a quilt-inspired design

Jenna was inspired by her grandmother's quilting and the uniforms of the men in the photo to create this star-pattern design. Mat photo and journaling block on blue cardstock; mount on 8¼ x 8¼" square cut from patterned paper (Anna Griffin). Double mat patterned paper square on red and green cardstock; mount in center of mustard cardstock. Punch four 1¼" squares from blue cardstock and four from green cardstock. Slice in half and arrange in quilt pattern. Accent with punched large stars (Family Treasures). Chalk edges of quilt elements and journaling block.

Jenna Beegle, Woodstock, Georgia

The Surgeon General releases a warning about the relationship between cigarette smoking and a variety of ailments, including cancer. The Federal Trade Commission requires all cigarette manufacturers to label packaging with a warning from the Surgeon General.

Cassius Clay (later Muhammed Ali) defeats Charles "Sonny" Liston to become World Heavyweight Champion.

Medicare is established.

President Lyndon B. Johnson orders U.S. bombing in North Vietnam after a U.S. military compound is attacked.

Malcolm X is killed in New York City.

Petula Clark records "Downtown," and the Rolling Stones record "Satisfaction."

Truman Capote publishes In Cold Blood.

In Miranda v. Arizona, the U.S. Supreme Court rules that an accused person must be informed of his rights before interrogation.

My Mother's Family
Craft a familial fan

Kimberly created this delicate fan, devoting one blade to each member of her mother's family. Mat photos with red cardstock; add gold corner stickers (K & Co.). Adhere gold border stickers (K & Co.), square sticker (K & Co.) and corners to background page. Draw one fan blade and trace it to create each additional blade. Completely affix bottom blade to page for stability. Poke through the bottom of all the blades with a fastener from a manila envelope; close fastener behind background page. Connect fan blades in back with thin strips of black cardstock. Mat photos and mount to fan blades. Decorate blades and fastener with stickers (K & Co., Stampendous!) and gold pen. Write journaling and title with gold metallic pen. Finish with letter stickers (Stampendous!) in title.

Kimberly Parker, Decatur, Alabama

(Shown with fan closed.)

Comstock

Preserve a portrait case

A frame may supply information about when and where a portrait was created. Mount open case on tan cardstock; mat again with red cardstock punched with decorative photo corner punch (Fiskars) and brown cardstock. Mount on patterned background paper (Design Originals). Print journaling (Creating Keepsakes) on tan cardstock; punch edges with pin hole hand punch (Fiskars) and mat on red cardstock. Freehand-cut tan and red cardstock border. Stamp border with feather stamp (All Night Media); heat-emboss half with gold embossing powder. Stamp and emboss two more feathers; silhouette cut and adhere to journaling block. Cut title letters from brown cardstock with template (EZ2Cut).

Oksanna Pope, Los Gatos, California

Sgt. Fred Robertshaw

Bust it up with a sewing machine

Julie's grandfather cut a dashing figure in his uniform. "It was no wonder my grandmother fell in love with him," Julie says. She created this equally dashing page by matting the photo on cream and dark blue paper and embossing the paper edges using the Empressor and Empressor Guide® (EK Success). Use a tracing wheel (available at a sewing store) to add "pin pricked" lines between the embossed pattern. Hand letter title and mat in cream and blue.

Julie McGuffee, Fort Worth, Texas

1967

Thurgood Marshall becomes the first African-American Supreme Court Justice.

The Beatles release "Sgt. Pepper's Lonely Hearts Club Band."

South African surgeon Christiaan Barnard performs the first human heart transplant.

U.S. population: 200 million

The Supreme Court strikes down sixteen state laws banning interracial marriages.

1968

North Vietnamese troops attack 100+ locations in South Vietnam, including Saigon, in the Tet Offensive.

Dr. Martin Luther King Jr. and Senator Robert F. Kennedy are assassinated.

Director Stanley Kubrick releases *2001: A Space Odyssey.*

A riot breaks out at the Democratic National Convention in Chicago.

Crimes of violence have increased radically—experts note a 57% in the past 6 years alone.

Williams
Unwrap a treasured photo

This unwrapped frame reveals a treasured photo from 1897. Create photo frame by cutting a 6½ x 8¼" piece of lavender card-stock. Cover with a 7¾ x 9¼" piece of patterned vellum; attach with heart brads. Create inner mat by backing speckled cream cardstock (Bazzill Basics) with lavender patterned paper (Paper Adventures). Slice a large "X" through both sheets of paper, extending incisions to within 1" of frame corners to form a window-like opening. Pull back flaps, attaching sides to background with silver brads and top and bottom with adhesive. Fold in ends and embellish with small ribbon bows. Freehand journal with gold gel pen; mat with clear vellum; apply small bow. Freehand title with gold gel pen on lavender paper and silhouette. Mount layout on olive cardstock.

Kathleen Childers, Christiana, Tennessee

Michelle Hubbartt, Grand Junction, Colorado

Our Family
Hang family portraits

Patterned paper with an agricultural theme pays tribute to hardworking ancestors. Triple mat photos with yellow and brown cardstock and patterned paper (Club Scrap). Attach gold eyelets (Creative Imaginations) at top corners; string with twine and hang from gold brads (adhere photos to background paper with adhesive to secure). Print title (Creating Keepsakes) and journaling on tan vellum (The Paper Palette); mat with tan cardstock and mount to patterned background paper (Club Scrap) with eyelets. Stamp wheat stamp (Club Scrap); silhouette cut and mount to photos.

Early 1900 Family Portrait
Create simple borders from patterned paper

Liane's strategically placed strips of patterned paper liven up this simple layout. Cover bottom half of background paper (Anna Griffin) with khaki paper. Cut three thin strips from another piece of the patterned paper. Adhere two strips to left and right sides. Adhere third strip an inch up from the bottom. Mat photo (cream mat is photo's original mat) on patterned paper (Anna Griffin). Embellish bottom with super jumbo fern punch (Punch Bunch). Adhere button. Make photo corners with corner pocket punch (Marvy/Uchida), covered with small fleurs-de-lis. Center mat on background. Print title on clear vellum. Embellish with punched fern branches and strips of olive paper. Print journaling on clear vellum, weaving cream and olive ribbon through top of journaling block.

Liane Smith, Gresham, Oregon

1969

American Neil Armstrong is the first man to walk on the moon.

Peace lovers celebrate three days of love and music at Woodstock.

President Richard Nixon announces the withdrawal of U.S. troops from Vietnam.

1970

National Guard troops open fire on antiwar protesters at Ohio's Kent State University, killing four students.

The Beatles disband.

Congress establishes the Environmental Protection Agency in July.

1971

Charles Manson and three followers are convicted for the murders of actress Sharon Tate and six others.

Richard Nixon agrees to visit the Soviet Union, which will make him the first U.S. president to do so since World War II.

"All in the Family" hits American TV airwaves.

Families Past
Curl torn edges with piercing tool

Curling the edges of this torn frame adds a more old-fashioned look to the photo. Mount photo to center of 9¾ x 8½" piece of paper. Cut same-size pieces of golden yellow and patterned paper (Making Memories), tearing out centers for photo frame. Use small, round tool, like a piercing tool, to curl the edges. Adhere golden yellow frame and then patterned paper frame over mounted photo. Adhere framed photo to background (Magenta) with foam mounting adhesive. Hang photo on gold brad by adhering fiber (On the Surface) to back of photo. Print journaling on cream paper.

Brandi Ginn, Lafayette, Colorado
Photos: Helen Bryant, Aurora, Colorado

Gertrude and Lorraine
Mimic intricate tile design

An antique tile floor in a restaurant inspired this border. Triple mat photo and adhere to green background. Print title and outline with green marker. Freehand journal. Double mat strip of cream paper for border. Create design by layering punched impatiens leaf under punched northern star (Emagination Crafts). Embellish leaf ends with small swirl punches. Punch cream and green mini quasars (Family Treasures) to complete design.

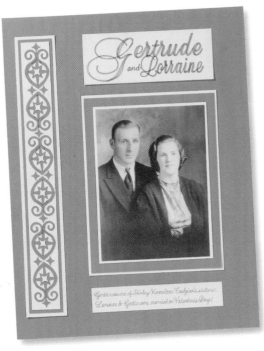

Paige Eliason, Gales Ferry, Connecticut

Oksanna Pope, Los Gatos, California

From Sea to Shining Sea
Pay tribute to courageous immigrants

Oksanna created a grateful tribute to her immigrant ancestors, who faced numerous hardships to reach America. Print journaling on white acid-free paper. Trim journaling block with Nostalgia paper edger (Fiskars); mat on blue cardstock trimmed with corner rounder punch (All Night Media). Decorate background with stars (All Night Media) punched from brush gold metallic paper (DMD). Print clip art of United States (IMSI) with title and subtitle on black cardstock; silhouette cut. Circle-crop two photos; mat on blue cardstock. Punch 4 x 12" strip of blue cardstock with film-strip border (All Night Media); weave with gold fiber (On the Surface). Trim other photos with Long Seagull paper edger (Fiskars); double mat with trimmed yellow cardstock and blue cardstock strip. Finish with handwritten names in black pen.

1972

Five men break into the Democratic Party National Headquarters in the Watergate offices in Washington, D.C. The Nixon administration denies any involvement. Nixon is re-elected.

Gloria Steinem founds *Ms.* magazine.

The New York City Court of Appeals upholds the right of a New York City woman to be a professional baseball umpire.

1973

Billy Joel releases his "Piano Man" album.

Arab oil-producing countries form the Organization of Petroleum Exporting Countries (OPEC) and refuse to export oil to nations that support Israel. An energy crisis begins in the U.S. and other Western nations.

Construction of the World Trade Center is completed.

Director George Lucas releases *American Graffiti.*

The American League decides to allow a 10th baseball player to bat in place of the pitcher.

The Henry Korthase Family
Save a signature

When creating a book about her husband's great-uncle, Hank, Jane decided to keep the layouts clean, simple and masculine; a strong signature became the perfect title. Scan photo in leather frame; print and mount to black background. Scan and print signature on yellow vellum; mat on white cardstock. Print journaling on yellow vellum; mat with white cardstock. Accent with heritage stickers (Me & My Big Ideas).

Jane Korthase,
Boyne City, Michigan

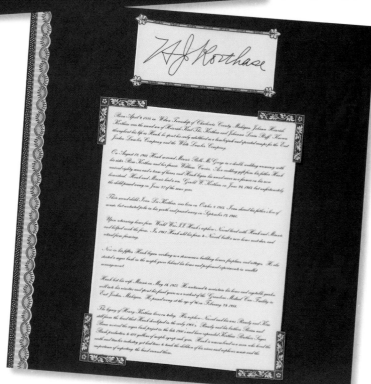

Young

Enhance with elegant, quilled embellishments

Quilled flowers accent the title and add to the vintage look. See instructions to quill your own accents. Fashion satin ribbon into photo corners and mat with striped, blue vellum (Hot Off The Press). Adhere to patterned background (Anna Griffin) with blue-flower eyelets (Stamp Doctor). Print journaling on white paper and adhere to background. Create border by matting strip of vellum with blue and white patterned paper (source unknown). Create title with Sizzix die cuts (Provo Craft/Ellison).

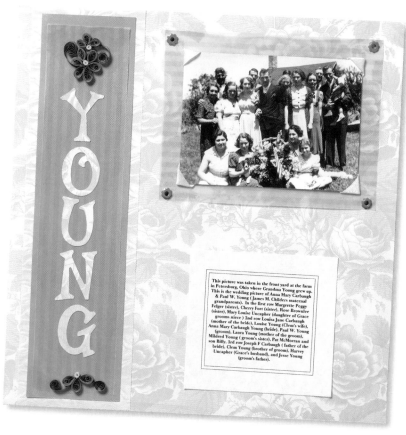

Kathleen Childers, Christiana, Tennessee

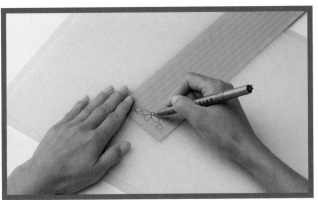

1. Draw desired pattern directly on matted vellum title strip using black marker.

2. Curl selected colors of quilling strips around quilling needle. Use a single strip of paper for each section of your flowerette. Glue loose ends to secure. Gently squeeze quilled circles into shapes needed such as tear drops.

3. Carefully glue quilled pieces on top of the drawn pattern, being careful to cover penned marks. Use tweezers to place pieces if necessary.

1974

After a televised impeachment hearing, President Nixon resigns. Vice-President Gerald Ford takes the oath of office. Ford pardons Nixon for any federal crimes.

Peter Benchley publishes *Jaws*.

Scientists announce that freon used in aerosol cans may damage the ozone layer.

Streaking reaches an all-time high.

1975

Director Steven Spielberg releases *Jaws*, a film based on the 1974 novel.

One Flew Over the Cuckoo's Nest wins Best Picture Academy Award.

The Bee Gees record "Jive Talkin'," their first disco hit. Beverly Sills debuts at The Metropolitan Opera.

The World population passes four billion.

The U.S. military academies allow women to enroll.

A two-hour period of prime-time television is set aside each evening for shows suitable for family viewing.

Christi Bobbitt, New Boston, Texas

1970s Flashback

Pick patterns appropriate to an era

When Christi saw these photos, she immediately "flashed back" to the vibrant colors and bright patterns of the 1970s. Crop photos and mat with patterned paper (Provo Craft); mount to patterned background paper (Provo Craft). Handwrite title on patterned paper (Keeping Memories Alive); mat on patterned paper.

Organizing Your Genealogical Research

To conduct successful genealogical research, you must be well-organized, so here are a few tips to help get you started:

First, separate your work into two different files: Original Files, which include birth/death certificates, marriage licenses, photos, letters, etc, never leave home. This helps assure their safety. Be sure to keep them in a secure place! The second category, Surname Files, are photocopies of your Original Files, plus notes and ideas for more research. These can be taken with you whenever necessary and written upon as needed. You may eventually need to create additional files, but these are good starting points for beginners.

With your organizational system in place, determine what branch of the family tree you'd like to research first and dive right in, tracing it back as far as possible. When you are finished, start over again using the same methods on another branch.

Keep in mind that the organizational process goes hand in hand with documenting your research: You can't document sources if you're not organized, and you can't get organized without documenting your sources.

1949

Emboss border for texture

This gold embossed border adds an ornamental effect and dimension. Mount olive background on slate cardstock. Trim 2½" strip of black paper with deckle scissors. Adhere to left side of olive background. For frame, stamp tan paper with Snow Bush stamp (Hero Arts). Once dry, use Kanji Poem stamp (Hero Arts) and black ink to vertically stamp over snow-bush design. Heat-emboss entire design with clear embossing powder. Cut into an 8 x 9⅞" frame for photo. Print journaling on parchment paper (Paper Adventures). Heat-emboss with clear embossing powder. Use scallop corner punch for green mat and mount journaling. For border, follow instructions below.

Amy Shibuya, Honolulu, Hawaii

1. Stamp the background paper using a fern-shaped stamp (Hero Arts) lightly coated with gold ink. Mask a portion of the stamp with removable artist tape to vary the length of the stamped image.

2. Once the primary images have dried, stamp additional leaves directly over previously stamped images using clear embossing ink. While still wet, apply gold embossing powder. Heat using an embossing gun to set the powder. This will cause your newly stamped images to rise slightly from the paper, giving them dimension.

3. Use scissors and a craft knife to cut along the edge of your stamped images, creating a border of overhanging elements. Add this border to your page.

Glossary

Acid-free

Look for scrapbook products—particularly pages, paper, adhesives and inks—that are free from harmful acids that can eat away at the emulsion of your photos. Harmful acids can occur in the manufacturing process. Check labels for "acid-free" and "photo-safe."

Archival quality

A nontechnical term suggesting that a substance is chemically stable, durable and permanent. Even if a product is labeled "archival quality," do not buy it unless it also says "acid-free, lignin-free and photo-safe."

Buffered paper

Paper in which certain alkaline substances have been added during the manufacturing process to prevent acids from forming in the future due to chemical reactions.

De-acidify

To chemically treat paper memorabilia to neutralize acids while applying an alkaline buffer to discourage further acid migration from damaging photos.

Encapsulate

To encase paper or three-dimensional memorabilia in PVC-free plastic sleeves, envelopes and keepers—for its own preservation and the protection of your photos.

Journaling

Refers to handwritten, handmade or computer-written text that provides pertinent details about what is taking place in photographs. Journaling can include various page accessories, such as stickers, die cuts, stamped images and punch art.

Lignin-free

Paper and paper products that are void of the material (sap) that holds wood fibers together as a tree grows. Most paper is lignin-free except for newsprint, which yellows and becomes brittle with age. Check product labels to be on the safe side.

Memorabilia

Mementos and souvenirs saved from travel, school and life's special events—things that are worthy of remembrance.

Page protectors

Plastic sleeves or pockets that encase finished scrapbook pages for protection. Use only PVC-free protectors.

Photo-safe

A term used by companies to indicate that they feel their products are safe to use with photos in a scrapbook album. Even if a product is labeled "photo-safe" do not buy it unless it also says "acid-, lignin- and PVC-free" as well.

Pigment ink

Pigment inks are water-insoluble and do not penetrate the surface being colored. Instead, they adhere to the surface, providing better contrast and sharpness. For journaling pens and inkpads, look for "acid-free" and "photo-safe" on the label.

Preservation

The act of stabilizing an item from deterioration by using the proper methods and materials manufactured to maintain the conditions and longevity of the item.

PVC or polyvinyl chloride

A plastic that should not be used in a scrapbook, it emits gases, which interact with and cause damage to photos. Use only PVC-free plastic page protectors and memorabilia keepers. Safe plastics include polypropylene, polyethylene, and polyester or Mylar.

Web Sites

ancestry.com: With a paid membership, you gain access to a database of information for 700 million names.

cyndislist.com: Cross-referenced links of hard-to-find categories such as Cajun heritage or convicts sent to Australia.

ellisislandrecords.org: Search for family members who entered the United States through Ellis Island from 1892-1924.

familysearch.org: Step-by-step research guidance and links to family history sites.

familytree.com: This page is a graphical index to genealogy Web sites.

genealogy.com: Good for beginners. Subscribe to World Family Tree to access research, search tombstones and connect your tree with famous families.

genealogy.about.com: A good place to read articles about genealogy. This site has helpful information on writing biographies and even has free heritage fonts.

genealogylinks.net: Links to sites for most nations of the world and the genealogy resources available for those countries.

genealogyspot.com: Easy-to-read gateway site to genealogy search engines. This one highlights Web sites that are worth your while.

maine.com/photos: This company offers photo restoration services. Their Web site includes information about the different processes and the differences between several kinds of old photographs.

nara.gov: Web site of the National Archives and Records Administration. Access to veterans records, government documents and more.

pbs.org/kbyu/ancestors/charts: Free forms to help organize your family research: pedigree chart, family group sheet, research questions and more.

rootsweb.com: Free searches and guides for tracing your family's movements.

tombstonesofthepioneers.com: Search through photos and the names on pioneer tombstones in the Southern states.

Books

Black Roots: A Beginner's Guide to Tracing the African-American Family Tree by Tony Burroughs. Details the best research techniques for collecting family histories, as well as getting through the myths, stories and omissions.

Everything Family Tree Book: Finding, Charting, and Preserving Your Family History by William G. Hartley. Learn to do research charts and records for accounts of your family's past. It includes a foldout tree chart.

A Genealogist's Guide to Discovering Your Female Ancestors by Sharon DeBarolo Carmack. A guide with plenty of tips on finding information about female ancestors.

A Genealogist's Guide to Discovering Your Italian Ancestors by Lynn Nelson. This book will help you find your Italian ancestors as far back as the 1700s without going abroad. Similar books are available for a variety of other ethnic backgrounds.

Genealogy Handbook: The Complete Guide to Tracing Your Family Tree by Ellen Galford. Hands-on resource shows how to use information you have and find more.

The Hidden Half of the Family: A Sourcebook for Women's Genealogy by Christina Kassabian Shaeffer. Turn to this book to get innovative ways of finding vital records of the past when searching for female ancestors.

How to Trace Your Family Tree by American Genealogical Research. Explains everything you need to know to trace your own family tree—how to begin, where to find help and how to organize your findings.

An Ounce of Preservation: A Guide to the Care of Paper and Photographs by Craig A. Tuttle. Filled with information on everything from protecting paper documents to recognizing, preventing and treating damaged photos.

To Our Children's Children: Preserving Family Histories for Generations to Come by Bob Greene and D.G. Fulford. A collection of more than 1,000 questions, offering a personal, human approach to genealogy.

Uncovering Your Ancestry Through Family Photographs by Maureen Taylor. A comprehensive guide to identifying the time, place and people in your old photographs.

Unpuzzling Your Past: A Basic Guide to Genealogy by Emily Anne Croom. A beginner's guide to starting your genealogy search. Includes simple forms for record keeping, a glossary of terms and an appendix listing research libraries and archives.

Writing Family Histories and Memories by Kirk Polking. Helps writers of all skill levels record their family histories.

Additional Instructions and Credits

cover Razoo Band

Jodi's grandmother took this picture, dubbing the ensemble the "Razoo Band." Trim ½" off 12 x 12" sheet of navy blue cardstock and use diamond border punch (Fiskars) around entire edge. Trim corners. Mat with red cardstock. Quadruple mat photo with white, gold, navy and red, using Clayson corner punch (Emagination Crafts) for navy mat. Print journaling on gold cardstock and mat with red. For title, cut music measure using a laser die cut (Deluxe Cuts) as a template and mat. Cut title with lettering template (Scrap Pagerz) from gold paper. Begin border by double matting a 1½ x 10½" strip of gold cardstock with navy and red. Adhere music charms (Elizabeth Ward & Company, Inc.) to 1½" navy squares with wire. Cut 2¼" red squares cut out of the middle. Adhere to blue squares with self-adhesive foam spacers.

Jodi Amidei, Lafayette, Colorado

page 16 Good Food, Great Friends

This spread's embellishments add so much texture, from the fibers and torn mats to the chalked paper roses. Begin by adhering block of lavender paper to center of patterned background (Magenta). Mat photos with torn vanilla paper. Print journaling on cream paper and adhere on left side. For title, use same font to print on lavender paper. Manipulate text with Word Art program so it prints backward. Cut out letters with craft knife. Thread four buttons with fibers. Attach to top through ⅛" holes and secure in back with thin wire. Dot a few spots of fiber with glue to spread the strands. For roses, coil green fiber for leaves, adhering as you go. Tear three circles for rose and chalk edges.

Brandi Ginn, Lafayette, Colorado

page 6 Carmella Teresa D'Angelo & Thomas Roland Ryan

The photo of Michele Gerbrandt's grandparents' wedding, taken in Pennsylvania in 1944, is spotlighted within a simple dark frame. Using a template, cut a large oval opening from a piece of 12 x 12" black paper. Trim 1½" from one side of paper edge; set aside the cut piece for later use. With a decorative corner punch, punch multiple designs from both black and cream cardstock. Adhere dark punched pieces to backside of frame, so the pattern extends inward. Adhere cream punched pieces to the backside of the trimmed paper edge with the pattern extending outward. Slip the narrow piece of black paper (trimmed earlier from the page edge) and slide it beneath the cream punched pieces. Adhere with photo tape. Mount photo. Journal on cream cardstock; mount with black photo corners and embellish with satin roses.

Pam Klassen, Westminster, CO

page 40 My Parents' Wedding

Victoria encased this layout in a shadow box to preserve the dimensional dress and tux. She had to adapt the layout to fit the shadow box's 16" height. Use two 4" strips of butternut color printed embossed vellum (K & Co.) to cover top and bottom of 12 x 16" piece of chip board. Center full sheet of background paper on chip board, overlapping the strips. Hide both seams with white tulle. Apply gold photo corners (Canson) to black mat and mount photo. Print title and journaling on vellum. Enlarge pattern from Shirts and Shorts Paper Folding (Design Originals), or create your own pattern for bridal attire. Detail dress by painting bodice and bottom hem with Opal Liquid Pearls (Ranger Industries) and then sprinkling with clear beads. Add white tulle to dress's skirt. Apply silk boutonniere to tux for extra flourish.

Victoria Jimenez, West Harrah, Oklahoma

page 58 My Army Days

Although Kelly's background is simple, her color scheme really makes her photos pop. Color block white background with burgundy, green, brown and burgundy textured (Faux Memories) paper. Mat photos and certificate, trimming some mats with deckle scissors. Print captions and journaling on vellum with Script font, trimming captions with deckle scissors. Mat journaling with cream paper and attach to background with pewter eyelets. Freehand title on vellum and detail with green gel pen. Adhere to background over green star die cut with eyelets. Punch three more stars. Adhere with eyelets and embellish two with fiber (EK Success).

Kelly Angard, Highlands Ranch, Colorado

page 74 Grandma's Hats

Carolyn's grandmother never went anywhere without a hat, and fortunately for Carolyn's scrapbook, Grandma Hoeflich loved having her picture taken! Mat small photos with ivory cardstock; mount on patterned background paper (Anna Griffin) over gardenia cutout (Colorbök). Print journaling on ivory cardstock; mat large portrait and journaling block on black cardstock. Mount embossed frame (Keeping Memories Alive) and gardenia cutout over large portrait. Finish with hat stamps (A Stamp in the Hand) on journaling block.

Carolyn Hassall, Bradenton, Florida

page 94 Generation 4 & 5

Nickie was lucky to find this text, an excerpt from a history book about Greene County, Iowa. Scan text into Word document. Use a desktop publishing program to create margin frame and to wrap text around photos. Print on embossed vellum (K & Co.). Use template (Creative Memories) to create decorative edges for corner accents on tulip-patterned embossed paper (K & Co.) and brown cardstock. Adhere corner accents to background (K & Co.), and then adhere vellum over accents. Print journaling with a frame. Double mat journaling and photo, adding triangles of patterned paper (K & Co.) to photo corners.

Nickie M. Hunter, Kansas City, Missouri

Professional Photographer

David L. Mishkin
Just Black & White
Portland, ME 04112
1-800-827-5881

Sources

The following companies manufacture products featured in this book. Please check your local retailers to find these materials. We have made every attempt to properly credit the items mentioned in this book. We apologize to any company that we have listed incorrectly or the sources were unknown.

3M Stationary
800-364-3577 3m.com

Accu-Cut®
800-288-1670 accucut.com
(wholesale only)

All My Memories
303-986-2200 allmymemories.com

American Greetings
americangreetings.com

American Tombow, Inc.
800-835-3232 tombowusa.com

American Traditional™ Stencils
800-278-3624 amtrad-stencil.com

Amscan, Inc.
800-444-8887 amscan.com

Anna Griffin, Inc.
888-817-8170 annagriffin.com
(wholesale only)

Artistic Wire artisticwire.com

Bazzill Basics Paper
480-558-8557 bazzillbasics.com
(wholesale only)

Boston International
800-637-5061 bostoninternational.com
(wholesale only)

Boutique Trims
248-437-2017 boutiquetrims.com

Boxer Scrapbook Productions
503-625-0455 boxerscrapbooks.com

Brodersbund
brodersbund.com

Canson, Inc.®
800-628-9283 canson-us.com

CARL Mfg. USA, Inc.
800-257-4771 carl-products.com
(wholesale only)

Carolee's Creations®
435-563-1100 carolees.com
(wholesale only)

Centis
888-236-8476 centis.com

Club Scrap™
888-634-9100 clubscrap.com

Cock-A-Doodle Design, Inc.
800-262-9727 cockadoodledesign.com
(wholesale only)

Colorbök™
800-366-4660 colorbok.com
(wholesale only)

Colors By Design
800-832-8436 colorsbydesign.com

Creative Imaginations
800-942-6487 cigift.com
(wholesale only)

Creative Impressions
Rubber Stamps 719-577-4858

Creating Keepsakes
creatingkeepsakes.com

Creative Memories®
800-468-9335 creative-memories.com

C-Thru® Ruler Company, The
800-243-8419 cthruruler.com
(wholesale only)

Cut-It-Up™
cut-it-up.com

CKC Creations, Inc.
888-451-8080

Dahler-Rowney USA
609-655-5252 dahler-rowney.com

Darice, Inc.
800-321-1494 darice.com

Deluxe Cuts™
480-497-9005 deluxecuts.com

Design Originals
800-877-7820 d-originals.com

DieCuts With a View™
877-221-6107 diecutswithaview.com
(wholesale only)

D. J. Inkers
djinkers.com

DMC Corp.
dmc–usa.com

DMD Industries, Inc.
800-805-9890 dmdind.com
(wholesale only)

Dover Publications
800-223-3130 DoverPublications.com

Duncan Enterprises
559-294-3282 duncan-enterprises.com
(wholesale only)

EK Success™
800-524-1349 eksuccess.com
(wholesale only)

Elizabeth Ward & Company, Incorporated
800-377-6715

Ellison® Craft and Design
800-253-2238 ellison.com

Emagination Crafts, Inc.
630-833-9521 emaginationcrafts.com
(wholesale only)

Ever After Scrapbook Co.
800-646-0010 everafterscrapbook.com

EZ2Cut Templates
260-489-9212 ez2cut.com

The Family Archives™
888-622-6556 heritagescrapbooks.com
(wholesale only)

Family Treasures, Inc.®
familytreasures.com

Faux Memories
813-269-7946 fauxmemories.com

Fiskars, Inc.
715-842-2091 fiskars.com
(wholesale only)

Frances Meyer, Inc.®
800-372-6237 francesmeyer.com

Gifted Line, The
800-533-7263

Gina Bear Ltd.
888-888-4453 ginabear.com
(wholesale only)

Graphic Products Corp.
847-836-9600 gpcpapers.com

Handmade Scraps, Inc.
handmadescraps.com
(retail only)

Hermafix (see Centis)

Hero Arts® Rubber Stamps, Inc.
800-822-4376 heroarts.com
(wholesale only)

Hot Off The Press, Inc.
800-227-9595 paperpizazz.com

Hyglo®/American Pin
800-821-7125 american-pin.com
(wholesale only)

Imaginations, Inc./O'Scrap!
801-225-6015 imaginations-inc.com
(wholesale only)

IMIS imsisoft.com

Jesse James Co.
610-435-0201 jessejamesbutton.com

JewelCraft
201-223-0804 jewelcraft.biz

K & Co.
888-244-2083 kandcompany.com
(wholesale only)

Keeping Memories Alive™
800-419-4949 scrapbooks.com

Lasting Impressions for Paper, Inc.
800-936-2677

Leaves of Time
888-409-2106 leavesoftime.com

Magenta Rubber Stamps
800-565-5254 magentarubberstamps.com
(wholesale only)

Making Memories
800-286-5263 makingmemories.com

The Marshall Company
800-621-5488 bkaphoto.com

Martha Stewart Omnimedia
marthastewart.com

Marvy® Uchida
800-541-5877 uchida.com
(wholesale only)

McGill, Inc.
800-982-9884 migillinc.com

Me & My Big Ideas
949-589-4607 meandmybigideas.com
(wholesale only)

Microsof
microsoft.com

Mrs. Grossman's Paper Co.
800-429-4549 mrsgrossmans.com
(wholesale only)

Nankong Enterprises, Inc.
302-731-2995 nankong.com

Northern Spy
530-620-7430 northernspy.com
(wholesale only)

NRN Designs
800-421-6958 nrndesigns.com
(wholesale only)

Offray & Son, Inc.
offray.com

On the Surface 847-675-2520

Paper Adventures®
800-727-0699 paperadventures.com
(wholesale only)

The Paper Company®, The
800-426-8989 thepaperco.com

Paper Cuts
888-337-0007 papercuts.com
(wholesale only)

Paper Inspirations®
406-756-9677

Paper Palette
808-595-3439

Paper Patch®, The
801-253-3018 paperpatch.com
(wholesale only)

Patchwork Memories
888-679-6560 patchworkmemories.com

Penny Black Ruber Stamps, Inc.
510-849-1883

Pioneer Photo Albums, Inc.®
800-366-3686 pioneerphotoalbums.com

Plaid Enterprises, Inc.
800-842-4197 plaidonline.com

Posh Impressions
800-421-7674 poshimpressions.com

PrintWorks
800-854-6558 printworkscollection.com
(wholesale only)

Preservation Technologies, L. P.
800-416-2665 ptlp.com

Provo Craft®
888-577-3545 provocraft.com
(wholesale only)

PSX Design™
800-782-6748 psxdesign.com

Punch Bunch, The
254-791-4209 thepunchbunch.com
(wholesale only)

Raindrops On Roses
919-571-9060

Ranger Industries
800-244-2211 rangerink.com

Robin's Nest Press, The
435-789-5387 robinsnest-scrapbook.com

Rubber Stampede
800-423-4135 rubberstampede.com

Sandylion Sticker Designs
800-387-4215 sandylion.com
(wholesale only)

Scherenschnitte Designs
509-486-8088 sdlcorp.com

Scrapbook Times
904-276-7990 scrapbooktimes.com

Scrap-Ease
800-642-6762 E-Craftshop.com
(wholesale only)

ScrapPagerz
ScrapPagerz.com

SEI, Inc.
800-333-3279 shopsei.com

Sizzix
866-742-4447 sizzix.com

Stamp Doctor, The
stampdoctor.com

Stampa Rosa, Inc.
800-554-5755 stamparosa.com

Stampendous!®
800-869-0474 stampendous.com

Stampin' Up!®
800-782-6787 stampinup.com

Sugarloaf Products, Inc.
770-484-0722 sugarloafproducts.com

Westrim® Crafts
800-727-2727 westrimcrafts.com

Whispers
602-469-2686 starlitstudio.com

Wintech International Corp.
800-263-6043 wintechint.com

Wordsworth Memories
719-282-3495

Wübie Prints
888-256-0107 wubieprints.com
(wholesale only)

Uptown Design Company™
800-888-3212 uptowndesign.com